T. & T. CLARK, EDINBURGH AND LONDON

I AM PERSUADED

IN GRATEFUL REMEMBRANCE

JOHN BAILLIE
HUGH ROSS MACKINTOSH

I AM PERSUADED

BY

The Rev. DAVID H. C. READ, D.D.

Edinburgh : T. & T. CLARK, 38 George Street

1961

PRINTED IN GREAT BRITAIN BY
MORRISON AND GIBB LIMITED
LONDON AND EDINBURGH
FOR
T. & T. CLARK, EDINBURGH

FIRST IMPRESSION . . . . . *September* 1961

CONTENTS

LINKED WITH THE TRINITY
OF LOVE

" And we have known and believed the love that God hath to us. God is love ; and he that dwelleth in love dwelleth in God, and God in him."—I JOHN IV. 16.

NEW YORK taxi-drivers, in the course of their daily business, must hear some strange conversations. Some days ago I was speeding down Park Avenue towards Grand Central Station with one of the Asian leaders of the World Council of Churches. We were having an animated theological discussion on what the Church ought to be saying to this modern world—whether it should chiefly be a message of hope, or of warning, or of exhortation, or of reproof. As we screamed round the curve towards the station, my friend came to the climax of his argument. " There's only one thing to say, only one thing to say to a world like ours : God loves you. That's all. That's what people need to know and that's what the Church has to tell them. God loves you."

" God loves you." This was not the opinion of a sentimental, unsophisticated Christian, inexperienced in the tough world of politics and business, untouched by the turmoil and terror of the last twenty-five years, unaware of the modern philosophies of despair. It came from a man who has lived through revolutions and wars, has visited nearly all the centres of world-power, and can hold his own with the theologians and philosophers of every school. Yet he feels that to-day the one central, decisive thing the Church has to say to the men and women of our era is just this : " God loves you."

You will notice that this is a statement—not a command ; a proclamation—not an exhortation. The world expects commandments from the Church : " Thou shalt love the Lord thy God . . . and thy neighbour as thyself ; " and appeals : " Come unto me . . . and I will give you rest." But, from the beginning, the first word of the Church is a statement : " God loves " : " God loves you " ; " God *so* loved that he gave . . ." That is the announcement ; that is the news : and from it flows the appeal, the commandment, the exhortation. As Christians, we fail in our duty to the world unless we give this news priority over all our appeals, and advice and rebukes. Only when a man or woman accepts and believes this tremendous statement can they begin to respond to the whole range of Christian faith and action.

There are indeed moments when there is little else to say. I read an article recently by a famous actress in which she tells how a minister rang her up to ask her to go and speak to a woman who was in a prison-cell, condemned for murder. She refused to go, on the grounds that she would have nothing whatever to say. Would you ? I couldn't go and say to a person condemned to death : " You ought to live a better life." Nor could I bring myself to say : " What you did was a terrible and wicked thing." But I believe that as a Christian I should have to find some way of saying the ultimate thing, the central thing, the all-important thing : " God loves you."

The man who wrote the words of our text is reputed to have been very old at the time of composing this letter. He had lived through the titanic struggle of the infant Church against the hostile powers of Roman imperialism and pagan philosophy. He had seen men and women of all ages tortured, and burned, and mauled in the arena for the sake of Christ. He had been through the struggle with the massive arguments brought by Cynics, and Stoics, and Epicureans, syncretists and agnostics, against the Christian Gospel. And it is recorded—that at the end, when almost unable to speak, he was carried in a chair to the congregation at Ephesus and was heard to repeat again and again : " Little children, love one another." In this letter he makes plain to the whole Christian world the basis for such a way of life. " Beloved, let us love one another : *for love is of God.*" " Herein is love, not that we loved God, but that he loved us." " We love him, because he first loved us." " God is love." The foundation for the entire structure of Christian faith and practice is this conviction that God is love, and that God loves us.

Yes : this is the first thing the world needs to know. Isn't it the same after all in a human relationship ? What does a young man want to hear, above all else, from the girl he wants to make his wife? A command ? Usually, poor soul, he's only too willing to hear and obey all kinds of commands—but that's not what he chiefly wants. An appeal ? Yes, let her make an appeal, and he'll come running—but that's not what he chiefly wants. Before all else he waits for one simple statement : I love you. It's when he hears and believes *that* that everything else really comes alive, and he's living in a new world.

In recent years we have been told often enough about the distinction between human and divine love. Congregations have been instructed about the Greek words Agapé and Eros—the first being the distinctive Christian word for the self-giving that is its heart, and the latter the common word for human love and desire. Yet we need to be reminded that this distinction is not absolute. While it is true that Christian love, God's love, is not primarily a matter of emotions —neither is the highest form of human love. The Bible is crammed with human love stories as it unfolds the drama of man's relationship to God—and there was even admitted to the canon of Holy Scripture that love-poem of sheer sensuous beauty known as " The Song of Solomon." The stories of love, and care, and affection ; generosity, loyalty, and self-sacrifice are in the Bible because they are part of *our* experience with one another : and they are in the Bible because, whether we know it or not, they are part of our experience with God. How often Jesus tells such a story of human love, and then directs our gaze to the heavenly Father with His majestic, " How much more ! "

" God is love." This statement appears on p. 1296 of my Bible, and so far as I know it is not to be found on any page before. The phrase is so familiar we might imagine the Bible to be full of it. But this is not the way these books are written. The Bible writers are concerned to show us God in action, not to make definitions. It is only when we have read the story of creation, the story of the call of Abraham, of the

Exodus, of the tumultuous history of Israel in its glories and miseries, expectations and disappointments ; when the word of the prophets has been heard ; when the four-fold tale of the Gospels has made its impression, followed by the account of the Early Church and the Epistles of Paul—it is only then as a climax that this short statement is allowed to break upon our minds and hearts : " God is love "—three monosyllables that changed the mental climate of the world.

These are the words that we take so lightly, such common coin in religious talk that we are almost ashamed to use them. It would do us good to remember that it was only after centuries of rough experiences with life as we know it ; only after the anguish of the prophets in the vortex of history ; only after the clouds of Calvary had descended on the agony of the Crucified ; only after the apostles and martyrs had blazed their way through hostile forces with their message of the Risen Christ—only then, that these words were written : " God is love." These words are not the opening words of a soft and comfortable philosophy of life : they are the final words of a rich and human testimony, written in the language of human sorrow and triumph, and sealed with the blood of martyrs.

" We have known and believed," says the apostle, looking back on all that has happened to him, to the Church, and to the violent world in which he lived. " We have known and believed the love that God hath to us." He is opening a door so that you and I can come in and share with him the experiences that led him to this ultimate discovery that " God is love." Shall we follow him as he leads us into the sanctuary of Christian faith ?

He begins where you and I begin—with the experience of love in a human community. There it is—in the family—the invisible power that holds it together and by which we later have grown up to be men and women. There it is—in the community, that group of friends, that fellowship, that service unit—again, a mysterious presence. No one can talk it down and say : " Look, here it is, the factor XPQ "—like one of those mystic compounds that is supposed to make one patent medicine so much better than all the rest. Yet we all know when it is present. We know it by the effects ; for the presence of love means cohesion instead of tension, a spirit of caring instead of callous indifference, and a readiness to put oneself in the other fellow's place.

No one should wish to claim that this Presence is the perquisite of Christians, and cannot be found outside their ranks. " God is love," says the apostle, " and he that dwelleth in love dwelleth in God, and God in him." That is surely a clear statement. We cannot delimit God's presence and say : here and here only is God to be found. He is found *wherever love is*. If a Christian group shows no love, no real caring, outgoing love—then God is not present whatever name the group may have. And if a family, a community shows real love, then God *is* present—even if there is no Christian profession in the group.

This is where we learn of love and where we learn of God. This Presence of love is the Holy Spirit in action. It is our first contact with the love of God whether we know it or not.

But the apostle went further as we who have heard the Gospel must go further. For what is the Gospel

but news about Jesus Christ, in whom the love of God
was focused to one turning point, becoming flesh to
dwell among us so that we can behold His glory ?
This we have " known and believed " if we are truly
members of His Church. We have seen Jesus and
watched the love of God in Him poured out in sacrifice
for men. " God is love " : yes, and " God so loved
the world, that he gave his only begotten Son, that
whosoever believeth in him should not perish, but have
everlasting life." If love is caring, who cared like
Jesus ? If love is outgoing, self-giving, who gave himself like Jesus ? If love is " putting yourself in the
other fellow's place " who ever carried this through to
the end like Him who bore our sins and carried our
sorrows, dying for us to bring us life ?

" We have known and believed the love that God
hath to us . . ."—the love we know alive in the world
by His Spirit, the love we see demonstrated in the gift
of His Son. Don't we also know and believe that
behind all things, and before all things is the love of
the heavenly Father ?

Once at a school conference I found myself faced
with the question : Why did God create the world ?
I suggested first that I myself would need to have
divine omniscience to answer such a question, but I
went on to make the only reasonable guess. " What
is behind human creation at its best ? " I asked, " the
impetus that inspires and creates a poem, a painting, a
garden, a ship, a home, a child ? Isn't it love ? Then
surely we can guess that the motive force that brought
all things into being—including you and me—was a
love pure and powerful beyond our dreams, the love
of the living God."

Thoughts like these lie behind our text—the love of

God the Spirit in our hearts and in human society ; the love of God the Son displayed in that amazing life and atoning death ; the love of God the Father, maker of all things visible and invisible. It is this that leads him to his great climactic statement : God is love— and with these words he carries us beyond this mortal scene, behind the silken curtain of Time, to that ineffable centre where our eyes are blinded by that Light that Milton calls " bright effluence of bright essence increate." Ineffable—that means that nothing can be said, yet can we not sense this about that inner life of God—that it is love, and since love is active not static, this love is the eternal, moving, on-going love of the Father, the Son, and the Holy Spirit ?

God is love. This is the foundation fact of the universe, this is the supreme discovery open to man. Yet it is not as a dogma, however important, not as a philosophy of life, however inspiring, that these words come alive for us. They reach us because you and I are drawn up into this Trinity of love. This is what brings high doctrine from the theological stratosphere to be a power in lives like yours and mine—even as the burning rays of a distant sun can be focused to light a fire for a June picnic. " God is love ; and he that dwelleth in love dwelleth in God, and God in him."

This is what happens in our worship and in our prayers. This is what happens when we open our lives to the Christian Gospel. The divine love seeks and finds us. The Holy Spirit is not simply a generating power of love in human society : He whispers in the secret place : God loves *you*. The Son of God is not simply the One who demonstrated for divine love once upon a time at Calvary. You realize He died for *you*.

The Father is not only the One who creates and sustains the fabric of the world : " He knoweth what *you* have need of before you ask." Thus, in spite of the sin still alive in our hearts, the evils and sufferings that surround us in the world, we can be linked with the Trinity of love, and know with all who believe that " neither death, nor life, nor angels, nor principalities, nor powers, nor things present, nor things to come, . . . shall be able to separate us from the love of God, which is in Christ Jesus our Lord."

II

UNCOMPLICATED CHRISTIANS

" But let your communication be, Yea, yea ; Nay, nay : for whatsoever is more than these cometh of evil."—MATT. v. 37.

THE first poem that I ever learned by heart as a boy, without being made to, was Macaulay's " Horatius at the Bridge " from his *Lays of Ancient Rome*. And I still remember the joy of declaiming the opening lines :

> " Lars Porsena of Clusium
>   By the Nine Gods he swore
> That the great house of Tarquin
>   Should suffer wrong no more.
> By the Nine Gods he swore it. . . ."

and so on it went, transporting me into a world of Roman heroism and romance. Lars Porsena, I suppose, attracted me right away by his magnificent capacity for swearing, " By the Nine Gods "—this was something beyond the experience of a small boy in Edinburgh ; this must have been a resounding and blood-curdling oath.

At that time I imagined, as many people still do, that when the Bible warns against swearing it refers to the vulgar or mildly blasphemous words with which we are tempted to express our irritation, or enliven an otherwise dull story. No doubt our Lord would have

something to say about this habit—and a good deal
more about our state of mind than the actual words
we use—but when He said " Swear not at all " He
was not referring to what we know as cuss-words, but
precisely to the kind of oath that Lars Porsena swore.
If Lars Porsena was going to take action on behalf of
the house of Tarquin all he had to do was to say so.
" But let your communication be, Yea yea ; Nay, nay."
What Jesus protested against was not the vehemence
of the language but the fact that a man feels it necessary
to underscore his simple word. That should be enough.

We are rightly scandalized to-day when a man or
woman lies under oath. Jesus was scandalized that
we should need to take an oath at all to prove that we
are not lying. With His rapier-thrust He cut through
to the fundamentals of human communication—the
plain, direct honesty of the word that corresponds to
the intention, the simple trust that we mean what we
say. In His Kingdom Yes means Yes and No means
No : and these words need no collateral.

It was very different in the world He lived in. In
those days there was a fascinating variety of names
by which a man could swear. To use God's sacred
name was, of course, the most binding. To swear by
heaven or earth was less so ; by Jerusalem less again,
and by one's head the least binding of all. Jesus
sweeps away these absurd gradations with the observ-
ation that they all really amount to the same thing—
namely, calling on the Creator as witness to one's
oath. For heaven is God's throne and earth His
footstool ; Jerusalem His holy city, and our heads
just what God has given us—" Thou canst not make
one hair white or black " (still ultimately, if not

cosmetically true !). His demand is that we use plain words that need no oath for reinforcement. Our text reads in the Greek quite simply : " Let your word be *Yes* or *No*." " Whatsoever is more than these cometh of evil."

Do you see what a light this throws not just on the ancient world of curious oaths but on the world in which we live ? For the blunt truth is that we can't get along without oaths and emphases and exaggerations and circumlocutions. The mere fact that a court of law requires a man to take an oath to tell the truth is an indication that society fears that normally a man will lie—to save his skin or his friends. The mere fact that you and I find it necessary to underline our commitments and refusals—" I will be *sure* to come to the meeting " ; " I 'll pay your bill *without fail* " ; " I love you *terribly, terribly much* " ; " I 'd simply *love* to come but unfortunately I may be prevented "— suggests that our Yes or No have slimmed away almost to nothing. If there were no evil in our human relationships, if everything were open and we had no guilty secrets, if the lines of communication between us were pure and uninterrupted, what a drastic simplification of speech there would be ! " For whatsoever is more than these cometh of evil."

The Sermon on the Mount reveals here, as elsewhere, the contrast between the clear bright light of God's Kingdom and the twilight world in which we actually live. Jesus knows all about this twilight world and He is not offering a series of rules and regulations to be immediately and literally adopted. Neither this word, nor the words about non-resistance, alms-giving, or divorce, can be made into a law that is binding on all Christians. Some have boldly attempted such literal obedience and have refused to take an oath in a court of law, as others have tried to isolate other sections of this teaching for literal application. But Jesus was not a legislator and in this twilight world He gave us not a law but a Spirit to live by—the spirit of an informed and understanding love. If I were to be rung up to-morrow morning by a gentleman in San Francisco who was willing to spend ten minutes of long-distance telephone time to try to persuade me to speak there at a conference next month, I should be acting entirely in literal obedience to our text if I said " Nay " and hung up. But something would be lacking in the sphere of Christian love !

2-   What good, then, does this teaching do ? Surely it has an immense relevance to our daily life by exposing the evil in which we are all involved, and pointing up the direction in which a Christian ought to move. ~~This is the Word of God to us, and " the word of God is quick, and powerful, and sharper than any two-edged sword, piercing even to the dividing asunder of soul and spirit, and of the joints and marrow, and is a discerner of the thoughts and intents of the heart."~~

Something is wrong with our " communication." That is obvious. We are far removed from a free and open encounter with one another that can be expressed by a clean Yes or No. When nations talk, the language of diplomacy wraps up agreements and refusals in an elegant package of circumlocution. When public figures talk, a thousand commentators are employed to speculate not on what they say but upon what they really mean. Advertisers have travelled so far from the land of Yea and Nay that we need a new vocabulary to interpret their claims. And preachers—yes, we

preachers are by no means exempt from the charge
of muddying the waters of communication and ob-
scuring the Yes or No of the Gospel in the complexities
of churchy gobbledegook.

Worse still is the complication of personal relations
in all areas, whereby friends and associates, employers
and employees, parents and children, even husband
and wife find road-blocks on the path of communication. Our trouble is so often our inability to express
ourselves, to reach the level of mutual trust symbolized
by this simple Yes and No. So we spin a web of words,
not so much to express, as to hide our real thoughts.

It is all so clearly pictured in the Genesis story of
the Fall. This is the pattern, ~~the archetype,~~ of all
breakdown in communication. The Garden of Eden
is the land of the clean and unadulterated Yes and No.
Man and woman are open to God, open to each other.
It is all simple and uncomplicated. Then comes the
serpent, and the whisper that sends up a little puff
of smoke—a tiny cloud of distrust and doubt—into
the clean air of the Garden—" Yea, hath God said
. . .? " When this has done its work, then trust is
broken and man can no longer look God in the face
and utter his simple Yes and No. " And Adam and
his wife hid themselves from the presence of the Lord
God amongst the trees of the garden." This is exactly
what we do. We hide ourselves in the foliage of the
garden which is the verbiage of our speech. No more
Yes and No. " Hast thou eaten of the tree ? " Yes ?
No ? Listen to him : " The *woman* whom thou gavest
to be with me, she gave me of the tree . . ." " And the
Lord God said unto the woman, What is this that
thou hast done ? And the woman said, The *serpent*
beguiled me. . . ." And so it goes—the verbiage of

self-excuse, the eternal passing of the buck. The triangle of trust—God, the man, the woman—is shattered with man's No to God, the links are broken, and he can no longer look either upward or outward with a clean conscience and an open heart. We are out of the garden of Yes and No, and the mighty gate has clanged shut behind us.

3 . The new life that Christ has brought to ~~mankind~~ *woman* has to do with exactly this situation. The new humanity He is calling into being is a family restored to the simplicities of trust in God and unclouded honesty among men. This is what He came to do. In His life men saw how uncomplicated it is to trust in the Father in heaven—" Have faith in God," " Your heavenly Father knoweth . . ."—and how simple is the compassion that offers a cup of cold water to the thirsty. In His words men heard again the mighty Yes and No on which our lives depend : " Blessed are the meek, the merciful, the pure in heart "; " Woe unto the proud, the hypocrites, the hard-hearted." As He swept the accumulated paraphernalia of religion from the Temple precincts and proclaimed the pure worship of God, so He swept aside the excuses and devices of a complicated piety and summoned men to follow Him into the kingdom of love. " Never man spake like this man." And wherever He has spoken since there has always been a mighty house-cleaning in the soul of man and a return to simple trust and love.

We are complicated Christians, most of us, to-day. We need to hear this word—" But let your communication be, Yea, yea ; Nay, nay," for our communication gets clogged and we cease to talk simply and honestly to God or to our fellow-men. Even in our religion we tend to make the Gospel a problem and the Christian life a series of dilemmas. God knows it is not easy to understand all the Bible has to say, and harder still to know just what is the Christian answer to the many problems of our day. But Christ did not come like the scribes to "bind heavy burdens and grievous to be borne, and lay them on men's shoulders." On the contrary, He said : " Come unto me, all ye that labour and are heavy laden, and I will give you rest." He does not give us rest from the task of understanding our faith and applying it to the life of everyday. But He does give us rest from the exhausting effort of hiding from God in the trees of our garden, and the nagging task of justifying and excusing ourselves before men. It is here at the centre He uncomplicates us and sets us on the path to the fullness of His Kingdom.

We have at home a large glass tank where some tropical fish are, I hope, reasonably happy. They flit in and out of little rocks amid a luxuriant foliage. Every now and then when I look at the tank I find the water cloudy and dull and the foliage rank and overgrown. Then next day the water is crystal-clear, the weeds trimmed back, and the fish darting about with all their colours radiant in the light and purity of their little world. What has happened ? Someone—not me—has cleaned the tank.

If I see a new clarity, a new simplicity, a new honesty in the world, in the nation, in the church, in the home, in my own heart, I know that someone—not me—has cleaned the tank. Christ is at work. This *is* His work—to uncomplicate us and bring us back to the simplicities of trust and love.

Whatever else seems hard—or even impossible—

about His demand for the pure and unadulterated Yes and No, there is one place where such a response is open to us all. It is His presence. When He says from the Cross : God loves you ; when He says by His Spirit : Come, follow ; when He says in His Church : Do you own Me Lord ? then " let your communication be, Yea, yea ; Nay, nay : for whatsoever is more than these cometh of evil."

The Gospel is God's great Yes to man—Yes, I will receive you and forgive you ; yes, I will empower you so that Christ will dwell in you ; yes, I will guide you through the rough and the smooth to the eternal Kingdom. But to hear that Yes, and to know its purifying power, we must utter our simple Yes to Him.

III

RATIONAL RELIGION

" And it came to pass, that, while they communed together and reasoned, Jesus himself drew near, and went with them."— LUKE XXIV. 15.

"WHILE they communed together and reasoned, Jesus himself drew near . . . and said : ' Stop reasoning ; you mustn't use your minds on sacred things. Faith is all you need.' "

Was that what happened ? If you remember the story of the two disciples on the road to Emmaus that first Easter evening, you will know that it turned out very differently. Perhaps you never noticed that these two disciples were reasoning. The Greek word that is used in the narrative is quite unmistakable. It means reasoning, arguing, discussing, disputing— the rational processes of the mind. That was what was happening at the very moment when the Stranger accosted them, the Risen Christ unrecognized. It was a religious discussion that was taking place on the Emmaus road, two minds at work on the same kind of problems that have often worried us—where God can be found in the events of our day, what is the meaning of the Cross of Christ, and what is the evidence that He rose from the dead. These two disciples are unknown. They might be you and me. Perhaps they are. What matters is that the Stranger makes no effort to stop the discussion. On the contrary, He joins it. " Jesus himself drew near, *and went with them*."

This is the true picture of the Christian faith. Whenever we genuinely exercise our minds on the great questions of human destiny, whenever we try to puzzle out what the Bible has to say, whenever we take religion seriously enough to try to think it through, Jesus Himself draws near and goes with us.

This is not quite the picture that we are given to-day. The reasoners are inclined to be left alone on the road to Emmaus, while Jesus is away on the mystic mountain-peak, or mixing with the crowds in some sentimental Galilee. It seems as though He has nothing to say to the reasoners except to tell them to be quiet. The suggestion is that rational processes have nothing to do with religion. Thinking is subversive to the Christian faith. And so the voice of the reasoner is drowned in the clatter of ecclesiastical machinery, the strident dogmatisms of electronic evangelism, or the lush appeal of escapist cults. It is as though we were afraid to let Christ come near these questioning minds of ours. He must be kept in some religious quarantine, sheltered among Gothic arches, praised in Gothic print, and spoken of in Gothic whispers. It is thus that we roll back the stone on that rocky grave, and isolate our Lord from the traffic of contemporary thought. Yet, again and again, in spite of our efforts, the Easter miracle happens. When minds are open and active, and truth is being resolutely sought, Jesus Himself draws near.

There are some welcome signs to-day that Christianity is again appealing to the mind of man. Far more books and plays with religious themes are being produced to-day than fifty years ago, and there has been a remarkable revival of concern for the Christian faith in the present student generation (much greater than among their older teachers). There is a growing recognition that the Christian Gospel offers more than an emotional satisfaction ; that it offers an interpretation of this mysterious world that is at least as rational as those secular philosophies whose bankruptcy is more apparent every day. A Christian college is no longer to be considered as a place where a modest secular education is dusted over with a little thin theology and irrelevant devotions. The colleges of our church are bold to claim the whole field of learning as the province of our God, and to believe that the Christian Gospel offers a better basis and perspective for a total education than any rival philosophy, hidden or acknowledged. The Christ, whom we have known to be the Way and the Life, is drawing near again as the Truth that satisfies the mind.

This is to return to the Bible, and to the finest traditions of our church. The God of the Bible speaks not only to the heart but to the mind of man—otherwise there would have been no such book. " Thou shalt worship the Lord thy God with all thy mind." With all its emphasis on the transcendent glory and majesty of God—" as the heavens are higher than the earth, so are . . . my thoughts than your thoughts "—the Bible never crushes the mind with an appeal to sheer irrational belief. " Come now, and let us *reason* together, saith the Lord." From the dust of conflict and trial we hear again and again the questions and arguments of the servants of God. We are given without apology the passionate cry of

Job, speaking for all anguished minds : " Oh that I knew where I might find him ! . . . I would order my cause before him, and fill my mouth with arguments."

It is sometimes supposed that the Christian Church set out as a group of ignorant men and women with a strong bias against the argumentative Scribes and Pharisees of their old religion and a fear of the rationalism of the surrounding culture of the Greeks. It is supposed that our Lord's appeal to become as children was a rejection of the adult mind, and that St. Paul's remark—" Where is the wise? where is the scribe ? where is the disputer of this world ? hath not God made foolish the wisdom of this world ? " —was a blanket condemnation of the intellectual. In fact neither Paul nor His master neglected the method of argument, and they showed the utmost respect for the serious questioner. We are told very clearly that thinking by itself will not get us into the Kingdom of God, and we are warned against pride of intellect and the folly of mere sophistication. But the New Testament is full of the word " understand." The Jews had to be led to understand, to understand how this Jesus is indeed the awaited Christ. And St. Paul would spend hours in a synagogue or by a river-bank patiently seeking to persuade. The Greeks had to be led to understand, and some of the apostles were willing to give time to learning to speak the language of the schools. And the vast questioning world beyond had to be led to understand. The voice of the whole thinking world sounds in the reply of the Ethiopian to Philip's question : " Understandeth thou what thou readest ? " " How can I, except some man should guide me ? " It was,

and is, the task of the Christian Church to be that
man.

As the Church gained strength and moved out into
the great cities of the ancient world, a tremendous
question had to be answered. We are all familiar
with the conflict between the Christian conscience
and the might of imperial Rome, and the ultimate
triumph of the martyr-spirit. We forget that other
conflict which was decisive for the influence of the
Church. For these men and women, mostly drawn
from the poorer and less educated classes, were faced
with the towering battlements of pagan philosophy
and schools of thought that were at many points
dramatically opposed to their dearest Christian convictions. They might well have decided to retreat
to their cells, ignoring the challenge, and damning
some of the greatest minds of their day with a sheer
irrational assertion of the Gospel. There were some
who wanted to do this—as there always have been
in the Christian Church. (It is much easier to tell a
man who does not have your faith that he is de-
ceived by the Devil than to try to understand his
arguments.) But, by the grace of God, there were
others in the Church who did not refuse the challenge.
They resolved that the pagan world must not be just
out-manoeuvred ; nor just out-lasted ; nor even only
out-loved : it must also be out-thought. And so they
set themselves to draw out the meaning of the Gospel
as an entire philosophy of life and to present it to
the pagan world as a rational and cohesive whole.
With all their imperfections these Fathers of the
Church so succeeded in their task that their Christian
philosophy was the basis on which European civilization was constructed and for centuries the thinking

of the Western world was dominated by the tenets of the faith.

Such a work cannot be done once and for all. Christ draws near to the pilgrim of the mind in every century, and inspires new men and women to wage the battle of the reason. Aquinas did it for the Middle Ages and left a mark on the thinking, and therefore the course, of the world for centuries to come. More than anyone else, John Calvin did it for the new age that dawned and his dedicated mind penetrated far beyond his native France, through the pulpits and people of Scotland, and Hungary and Holland and a dozen other countries, to the very Constitution of the United States.

We stand in a tradition of rational religion. That is not the whole story, but it is a part of which we need to be reminded. Every time we speak in disparagement of the place of the mind in the Christian Gospel, every time we are tempted to give up the struggle to make sense of our beliefs in the light of contemporary knowledge, any time we withdraw into a soft and sentimental religiosity, we are betraying the work of our own Christian ancestors. It was John Knox—that thunderous preacher of a sovereign God whose thoughts are not our thoughts—who drew up the first plan ever made for having a school in every parish of Scotland. It was our Christian ancestors here who inspired the founding of colleges long before government or any other power was interested. Christian colleges in India and Africa have played, and are playing, an immense part in shaping the destinies of a future world.

"And it came to pass, that, while they communed together and reasoned . . ." They are communing together and reasoning out on the roads of Asia and Africa and India to-day. Ideas are flowing across the world and decisions are being made. Do we, as Christians, get into this conversation, or are we content to let it be fed by secular ideas and materialist dialectic ? Wherever the Christian Church—the Body of Christ—(and that means you and me) is awake to this task and ready to respond, it can be said again that " Jesus drew near and went with them."

They are communing and reasoning on the campuses and in the schools of this country. They are communing and reasoning in clubs and apartments, in theatres and libraries, in radio and television in this our city. Are we—the Body of Christ—prepared to draw near and go with them ? Or do we withdraw, and close up when religion is mentioned because we have not thought through the reasons for the faith that is in us ? The battle of the mind never stops and never was it more decisive than to-day. What a task for a church ! It is thrilling to think that there might be a boy or girl in our Church School whom God has chosen to write that book or that play that will swing the minds of millions now alive towards the acceptance of Lordship of Christ.

Rational religion ? I can almost hear someone protesting : do you mean then that our task is to make our religion acceptable to the modern mind, to concentrate on rational arguments, and to eliminate all that is offensive to our unbelieving friends ? No, indeed : that is *rationalist* religion, which is a very different matter. Rational religion recognizes the place of the mind : rationalist religion thinks there is nothing else that matters. Rational religion seeks to understand : rationalist religion believes that all our understanding is done with the mind. Rationalist religion is a thin and dry diet for a hungry soul. Christianity is rational, not because you can be argued into accepting it, but because it is prepared to give reasons ; and because, once accepted, it offers a more rational view of the world, I believe, than any rival philosophy.

Once accepted—that is the whole point. Why do we accept ? Well, whoever we are, and whatever we believe about the ultimate questions of life and death, we are accepting some philosophy of life. We can't help it. And, whatever it is, we do not accept it on wholly rational grounds. No one can mathematically prove the truths by which he surely lives. The most sceptical point of view still demands an act of faith. Atheism requires as much non-rational acceptance as religious belief. (You can see this in the passionate atheist who is like a fervent Christian believer standing on his head !) Acceptance comes with the presence of that which goes beyond our reason. To go beyond is not to deny : it is only beyond that reason finds its wholeness and its home.

The presence from beyond. There was such a presence on that Emmaus road. But, for the moment, they did not know. Like us they continued the discussion, trying to think their way through, as they walked through the dusk towards the twinkling lights of a distant inn. There was so much still to be answered, and almost without looking they drew the Stranger into their debate. Their eyes were on the road ahead, the road of argument, the turns and twists of reason, the deceptive short-cuts, and the long dusty straight. On such a path " their eyes were holden that they should not know him." That

I.A.P.—3

is what it says—right after our text. " Their eyes were kept from recognizing him."

I have sat through debates and discussions where men of goodwill, but no religious faith, were thrashing out the great problems of our destiny. And I have been aware of a presence from beyond, of the Stranger who was making His secret contribution to the talk, yet " their eyes were kept from recognizing him." Sometimes it is we ourselves, through our weakness and folly, who get in the way. Sometimes it is because men walk with the blinkers of rationalism and are blind to all the other avenues of truth that impinge upon the human spirit. They become insensitive to the Presence—afraid perhaps of what may happen when a disturbing Power gets in among the maps and blue-prints of the mind. And yet this is the logical end of the rational process—the recognition of the boundaries no mind can cross, the humble waiting for the word from the other side.

It sometimes happens that such a word comes to us from an unexpected direction. A familiar verse of the Bible takes on new meaning ; the chance remark of a friend opens a little door in the mind ; an unaccountable instinct leads us to worship where we have not been before ; a sound, a shape, a touch —and it is like hearing the distant music of church-bells over the fields of memory. The Stranger is drawing near. This is the moment when the merely rational is transfused with a stronger light—and it is a moment that we must not lose.

" He made as though he would have gone further. But they constrained him, saying, Abide with us : for it is toward evening, and the day is far spent." Perhaps it is when we begin to realize that the day is

far spent that we begin to need that Presence most.
But any time—and the sooner the better—we can
detain the Stranger and invite Him in.

What was the end of this long road of discussion
and debate ? A very simple meal. Bread and wine
on a table do not need a vast intellect to comprehend.
They speak from the elemental depths of this earth
we live on, and the sharing at the table is the com-
monest expression of our mingled lives. " And it
came to pass, as he sat at meat with them, he took
bread, and blessed it, and brake, and gave to them.
And their eyes were opened, and they knew him."

This is the Light that breaks in on our perplexities
and discussions. It is not a glaring and blinding light
that reduces our reasonings to nonsense and evokes
a quite irrational response. It is the Light that comes
when talk is through, when we have reached the
borders of our human thinking, and are ready to
acknowledge the presence of the beyond.

This is the Christ of God—the source of all wisdom,
the Light in which we see light—who comes in the simple
elemental things—a song, a prayer, a handclasp, a
cup of coffee, a loaf of bread—to open to us a Kingdom
that lies beyond the limits of our minds.

IV

WHERE GOD IS TO BE FOUND

" For thus saith the high and lofty One that inhabiteth eternity, whose name is Holy ; I dwell in the high and holy place, with him also that is of a contrite and humble spirit, to revive the spirit of the humble, and to revive the heart of the contrite ones."
—ISA. LVII. 15.

THIS is the time of the year that makes us say to ourselves : " Wouldn't it be nice to be like one of these sensible animals that goes to sleep when the snow is on the ground and wakes up with the leaves and the flowers, and the sunshine of spring ? " And yet we know very well that a good part of our joy in the Spring depends on our experience of winter. The satisfactions of life are so often dependent on a preceding discipline and privation. Hunger is, we know, the best sauce for a good meal ; and every smoker knows that a pipe, a cigar—or even a cigarette—tastes the better the longer we have been without one. There is no by-pass road to our human joys and satisfaction.

So it is in our Christian life. The pinnacle of joy and satisfaction in our faith is our communion with the Risen Christ. To know this Lord who has broken the powers of evil, to be united with this Lord who has undergone the sharpness of death and opened the kingdom of heaven to all believers, to sing with the Church Universal " The strife is o'er, the battle done . . .," to be confident that " neither death, nor life, nor things present, nor things to come shall be able to separate us from the love of God which is in Christ Jesus our Lord "—this is indeed the summit of the Christian life on earth. And we should all like to get there right away. Let modern man have but an inkling of what this is, give him just a passing glimpse of the joy and peace that comes with confidence in the Risen Christ, and he will bare his arm for a shot. " Give me the Easter needle ; inject something of this radiant belief into my wilting spirit and jaded nerves ! " But there is no Easter needle. There is, instead, a pilgrimage—a way to be followed that leads to our summit meeting with our Lord.

To be a Christian is to follow Christ—and for Him there was no leap from the stable of Bethlehem to the Resurrection Garden. The Christian creed does not run straight on from " born of the Virgin Mary " to " on the third day he rose again from the dead." " He suffered under Pontius Pilate, was crucified, dead and buried ; he descended into hell." No one has ever reached the summit of communion with the Risen Christ, and known the confidence that He is Lord of life : death : conqueror of sin : without going with Him in some measure through the shadows of suffering, without knowing at least a little of His hell of loneliness and pain.

And so it is good that there should now stretch before us the six weeks of Lent. There should be nothing artificial about this. We are not acting a part—pretending for six weeks that Christ has not really risen from the dead. But we are given this period to think of those things that made Easter possible, those things that made Calvary inevitable—our situation as wandering, confused, and sinful men and women searching for a God in whom to trust. If we have never given time and thought to our condition of estrangement from one another and from God, if we have never cried with Job, " Oh, that I knew where I might find him ! ", or confessed with Daniel, " O Lord, to us belongeth confusion of face, to our kings, to our princes, and to our fathers, because we have sinned against thee "—then we cannot truly hear the Voice that calls from the vortex of our human struggle : " I am the resurrection, and the life." We do not really envy the hibernating animal who emerges to blink in the sunshine he cannot really understand ; nor can we envy the hibernating Christian who appears at Easter to celebrate a triumph he will never truly know.

The central question with which we are concerned, the question to which Easter gives the final answer, is that of knowing God. And it is this I want to think about with you on this first Sunday of Lent. Knowing God. Finding Him. Being related to Him as we are to one another. Where is He ? How do we reach Him ? What kind of thoughts should we have about Him ?

If I wanted to know about the nearest planet to this earth, how to find it with a telescope, and what the chances are of a personal visit in my lifetime, I should consult the best scientific authority available. I wouldn't be content with the opinions of my friends on the matter. I wouldn't go to the poets or the artists. I wouldn't consult the prophet Daniel or approach the Book of Revelation with a bent pin. And so, if I want to know about God, I listen to the best authority, the record of men who found Him and knew Him— not in some abstract philosophic formulation—but as a living factor in our human situation, as a Person active in and beyond this world we know. Such an authority speaks in our Bibles, and its word is backed by the experience of millions of people like ourselves. There is such a voice of authority, speaking out of a time of bewilderment and confusion not unlike our own. Where is God to be found ? " For thus saith the high and lofty One that inhabiteth eternity, whose name is Holy ; I dwell in the high and holy place, with him also that is of a contrite and humble spirit, to revive the spirit of the humble, and to revive the heart of the contrite ones."

1. " For thus saith the high and lofty One that inhabiteth eternity, whose name is Holy ; I dwell in the high and holy place . . ." Have we heard that ? This is the God with whom we have to do. He inhabits eternity. His name is holy. He dwells in the high and holy place.

What do we know of the high and holy ? These are words that cannot be defined. They are like signposts standing at the edge of our everyday experience pointing to the infinite beyond. The high and the holy cannot be trapped by our human skills, measured by our instruments, or harnessed for our use. The God who dwells in the high and holy place is a God who cannot be defined by human reason, or enlisted for our human enterprises. He who inhabits eternity cannot be just one other object to be discovered by the human brain. Therefore His existence is not something to be proved by human arguments or demonstrated by the instruments of science. To say this is not to retreat into sheer fantasy and religious imagination. For the mystery of God's existence has a parallel in your own existence. You cannot use your brain to prove your own existence. You can, as it were, step aside and watch yourself existing, but there is still the " you " that is doing the watching—mysterious, uncapturable, never to be found, yet most truly there. The God of the high and holy place is surely not less elusive than your mysterious self. And so it is that of all the possible human language-symbols to give a name to God, the Bible finds in the end nothing else than this— the Hebrew verb that means I AM—JAHWEH, " I AM THAT I AM."

" I dwell in the high and holy place." Sometimes people speak to-day as if the God of the Bible were a kind of simple projection of man's needs, a father-figure who dwelt in the imagination of primitive man —and nowhere else. And at times in the church we encourage them to think this way. We talk of a God who is as readily available as a telephone operator, a God at the mercy of our human discoveries, a God so tied to our solid earth that if it were to disappear He would disappear with it and be swallowed up in outer space. We are, in fact in danger of making space our God and thinking that the Bible-God, the God of our fathers, is imprisoned with mankind. And so in our worship we appear to offer something like that little metal cage in which a brave man recently spent seven days of simulated flight through space. We close the door and shut ourselves off from the world : we hear the voices of eternity but when we emerge it is evident that we have never left the solid earth. To hear the authentic Word of God—" I dwell in the high and holy place "—is to be delivered from such earth-bound worship, to realize afresh that the God of the Bible is one who holds all space in His control. " I have made the earth, and created man upon it : I, even my hands, have stretched out the heavens, and all their host have I commanded." It is to realize that the God of the " high and holy place " is the God who summons us to a worship that really touches the eternal, and in whose immensity our human thoughts find rest. " For my thoughts are not your thoughts, neither are your ways my ways, saith the Lord."

" Neither your ways my ways." God is not only in the high place beyond our thinking : He is in the holy place beyond our utmost striving. Isn't one of the reasons why the Christian Gospel has less grip on us than we feel it ought to have simply that we have lost the sense of the holiness of God ? We can sing " This is my Father's world " and feel a sense of confidence and peace ; but how much does it mean when we sing : " God reveals His presence : Let us now adore Him, And *with awe* appear before Him " ? It was when the young Isaiah really knew the presence of God and heard the song of the seraphim, " Holy, holy, holy, is the Lord of hosts," that he cried : " Woe is me ! for I am undone ; because I am a man of unclean lips . . ." It was when Peter glimpsed the holiness of God in the face of Jesus Christ His Son that he cried: " Depart from me ; for I am a sinful man, O Lord."

We are aroused to awe and wonder as we peer out to the distant spaces and ask ourselves what mysteries they may hold for man. We know what it is to say with Pascal : " The eternal silence of these infinite spaces frightens me." How do we feel in the presence of the living God who dwells in the high and holy place ? For it is with Him we have to do, not with the vast anonymity of the stratosphere. Just as the earth controls its satellite, and is itself the satellite of the

sun, and the sun a satellite of the solar system, the
solar system a satellite of some immensity beyond, so
the entire universe is a satellite of our God. And this
is the high and holy One who inhabits eternity from
whom we came and to whom we go.

Where is He to be found ? In the high and holy
place. Is this equivalent to saying He cannot be found
at all ? No ; for every one of us here this morning
has caught at least the echo of His voice. Our farthest-
ranging thoughts have touched their resting-place in
Him. Our deepest aspirations have been the signposts of eternity. Our conscience acknowledges His
holiness. In the depths we know what it is to hear the
Voice : " Be still and know that I am God."

2. God can be found. There is only one way in
which people like you and me can know the One who
inhabits eternity—and, thank God, it doesn't depend
on our intellect, our position in life, our mystic capacity,
our talents, or our goodness. " Thus saith the high
and lofty One that inhabiteth eternity, whose name is
Holy ; I dwell in the high and holy place, *with him
also that is of a contrite and humble spirit*."
Every great discovery depends on using the right
methods. If I want to discover how to reach the
moon I must use the science of ballistics. If I want to
discover the beauties of painting I must go to school
with the great artists. If I want to discover the joys
of human love I must know how to open my heart to
another. Of all these it is the discovery of human love
and friendship that is the nearest parallel to knowing
God. To know Him I must open my life. And what
does it mean to open my life to the high and holy God ?
It means that I do not shut the doors of mind to His

presence, or fill my life with so much rattling busyness
that His voice is drowned. It means that I am awake
to His presence as the high and holy Third when I
discover human love. It means that I make room for
worship and for prayer.

And when I do, what happens? Perhaps it seems
that nothing happens. For the moment we have an
inkling of the high and holy God we seem more feeble
and lost than ever before. He is high—I cannot reach
Him. He is holy—my best is so shoddy it cannot bear
the light. Do you ever feel that way? The most high
God makes you feel so very low, the holy God so sinful
and ashamed. If you do feel this then your search is
ended. For this is the way God reaches to the human
heart. " I dwell in the high and holy place, with him
also that is of a contrite and humble spirit." To be
humble and contrite is not to crawl around with
ostentatious meekness and unwilling remorse. It is
that inward fasting of the spirit that in the lonely depth
of our real selves is humble before the most high, and
contrite before the most holy.

Where is God to be found? In the high and holy
place which is the refuge of our thoughts and the
strength behind the fabric of the universe. Yes, and
also, and just as really, in the contrite and humble
heart.

Since Jesus walked in Galilee there have been many
pages of turbulent history. Empires have risen and
fallen, kings and dictators have come and gone.
Century after century the spirit of man has gone
questing after truth, " voyaging through strange seas
of thought alone." And to-day we are again out on
the restless oceans of new discovery and new danger.
There is one constant factor behind the shifting story—

the will of the high and holy God. And there is one
constant redeeming grace made possible for all—to be
humble and know we are not God, to be contrite and
know we are not good. This is to know the living God.

"The tumult and the shouting dies ;
  The captains and the kings depart :
Still stands Thine ancient sacrifice,
  A humble and a contrite heart.
Lord God of hosts be with us yet,
Lest we forget—lest we forget ! "

VI

GOOD AND BAD: THE GIFT OF DISCERNMENT

" Give therefore thy servant an understanding heart to judge thy people, that I may discern between good and bad : for who is able to judge this thy so great a people ? "—I KINGS III. 9.

IT was a dream—this encounter between Solomon and his God. Like many dreams it was distilled from the fears and sense of inadequacy that had suddenly possessed him. For years he had looked forward to the moment of his coronation. He had been intoxicated with the dazzling prospect—the power and prestige of kingship, the glitter and glory of the throne. And now that it had come somehow the romance was fading and he was face to face with the responsibilities of his office. He knew now that he would have to make decisions—decisions that would affect thousands of his subjects, life-or-death decisions, peace-or-war decisions, decisions between policies, decisions between people. And for all of them, in the last resort, he would be alone. No wonder he carried his anxiety to bed with him, and dreamed himself into the presence of his God. At this point he needed as never before the presence of a mind greater than his own, the resources of a Goodness beside which he felt naked and ashamed.

This is the natural response of a man of conscience thrust into a position of power. I imagine that a President of the United States has a similar sensation

47

after the tumult and glamour of the election is over. But it's not only such high offices that bring this desperate sense of need. Every one of us has known the sudden thrust of responsibility that makes us quail. A new job looms up—perhaps one we have long desired : and the excitement of getting it is soon followed by the disturbing whispers : " More responsibility ; fewer people to fall back on ; more dependent on me ; have I got what it takes ? " Or, think of a bride : here is the climax, the fulfilment of her dreams (" even Solomon in all his glory was not arrayed like one of these ! "), and yet it is a singularly thoughtless girl who does not also tremble a little at the thought of the vast new responsibilities and decisions that lie ahead. So it is with the arrival of a baby. When the proud father has recovered from the excitement and the joyful sense of fulfilment he must surely look down at that tiny bundle of life committed to them both, and wonder : " How can I do what is best ? A life—and I am responsible. My decision now will echo through the years. Where can I turn for help ? "

When we are in this kind of position—as we all are from time to time—it is natural to turn to prayer. For some of us this kind of crisis is often the first real impetus towards a personal faith in God. The new situation, the new responsibility, has shown us a need that we had scarcely been aware of before. What has happened is that some of the protective bulwarks have been torn down—the fortification provided by others who used to take decisions for us, the sheltering circumstances of our simpler life. We are now on our own, and to be on our own is to know our deepest need—our need for a guiding God.

" The Lord appeared to Solomon in a dream by

night : and God said, Ask what I shall give thee."
" Exactly," says the sceptic. " This guiding God of
yours is a dream. You Christians suffer from a sense of
inadequacy and fear of responsibility, so you dream up
a Father-figure to take care of you. Your God is just
Santa Claus with religious trimmings, and your prayers
and worship a method of persuading Him to tip some
gifts out of His sack."

All right, this *was* a dream that Solomon had. And
the Bible tells us it was a dream. The writers of the
Bible are quite capable of distinguishing between
dreams and reality. There are some definite dream-
features in this picture of Solomon's talk with God.
The Lord appears, as it were, holding behind His back
a whole collection of gifts and He says, " Now choose
the right one—and you'll get the lot." Solomon's un-
conscious throws the whole episode into the form of a
quiz and give-away programme. He hits on the right
thing to ask for—" an understanding heart "—and he
collects the lot—riches, honour, prestige, length of days.

We should be foolish to imagine that this dream
element disposes of the truth and practical relevance
of the story. Solomon is in the dream—and he is a real
person. So is God. And what we are being permitted
to overhear is precisely the way in which a real God
responds to the need of a real man in desperate need of
guidance. And when we discover how He does respond,
when we think again about the nature of the gift that
is granted we shall see that the whole point of the story
lies in the fact that God does *not* act like Santa Claus ;
He does *not* respond to a demand for quick answers and
success. He is *not* a dream-figure on to whom we shift
our responsibilities. He is the One who sends us right
back to face our own problems, and make our own

decisions—with the one gift that will not destroy our human stature, an " understanding heart."

It is a caricature of true religion that paints it as escape from the hard facts of life. It is precisely the opposite. The God of the Bible doesn't promise us any short-cuts to success. Instead He shows us the only road that makes sense of all the factors in this mysterious world and offers us His companionship on every stretch, uphill, downhill, along the flat, and round every corner. Our prayers are not meant to save us from decisions but to provide the light in which to make them. He does not give us end-results but the strength to reach them. He provides the instruments and the inspiration—not a recorded symphony ready to be enjoyed. The believer is like a sculptor facing a solid block of marble. He doesn't pray to some dream-God to transform that block into a perfect, finished statue before his eyes. Nor does he give up in disgust at his inadequacy and make for the nearest bowling-alley. He meets the challenge of the marble, knowing that this is what he was born to do, and that the creative Spirit that gave him life can work through him towards a perfect end. For a true Christian God is not the magician who saves him trouble. He is the divine source from which we draw the wisdom and the courage to face life as it really is.

Here then is the best prayer we can make. " Give therefore thy servant an understanding heart . . . that I may discern between good and bad."

When we learn to pray this prayer we are really on the Christian road. Our religion ceases to be escapist and becomes what it ought to be—the light by which we really see—the power by which we truly live. The characteristic of all the finest Christian men and women who have ever lived has not been their outstanding success, their dominating personalities, their brilliant minds. It has been their understanding hearts.

1. An understanding heart means, in the first place, just what our text says it means—being able to discern between good and bad. The Revised Standard Version translates " an understanding *mind*," for in Hebrew psychology the heart was the instrument of thought as well as feeling. We are not dealing here with vague sentiments about goodness, but with the hard practical daily task of distinguishing between good and bad. This is the gift we are to seek from God. Those who seek it are the realists—they know what life is about. Those who avoid it are the escapists—they will not face the major decisions that confront us day by day.

" Discerning between good and bad." There are signs that we are busily engaged in dodging this issue at this very time. Semantic signs, in the first place. The very words " good and bad." are being squeezed out of our vocabulary. We have become so impressed with the fact that " there's so much good in the worst of us and so much bad in the best of us " that we have lost touch with the ultimate distinction. So we begin to use different words. For " good " we substitute pleasant, helpful, well-adjusted, well-rounded ; for " bad," unpleasant, unhelpful, maladjusted, sick, disturbed. (What our grandfathers called a " bad boy " is now a " maladjusted juvenile delinquent.")

All this may be a sign of increased understanding as revealed by the vast improvements in our treatment of crime and mental disease. But it may also be a sign of the moral relativism that is destroying the fibre of society. Good and bad, many have come to believe, mean little more than " I like it " and " I don't like it." A whole school of philosophy has arisen to tell us that " good " and " bad " are really no more than grunts of approval or disapproval. And it is a common experience for many of us to be told by a college boy or girl that there is no absolute good or bad—only shades of opinion, varying from place to place and year to year. (If you press them with the question : " Are you *sure* there are no absolutes ? " they will say yes ; but if you go on, " Are you absolutely sure ? " they begin to think again about the whole question !)

There is another pressure on us to-day that works against our discriminating between good and bad. Evil, in our generation, has assumed such monstrous proportions in certain areas that our consciences are numbed. The simple and passionate judgments of good and bad in human affairs in days when wars, and revolutions, and massacres, were on a limited and local scale, have become completely muted under the shadow of the missile and the bomb. Because most of us don't see a way out of the dilemma of having to resist a totalitarian system we recognize as evil by methods we know also to be evil, we are in danger of losing altogether our discernment of good and bad, and of calmly acquiescing in a *status quo* of murderous possibilities for the human race. To have an " understanding mind " does not mean that we have some simple solution to propose. It does mean that we cannot escape to some private " peace of mind " in a world where one half of the population is starving while the other half prepares mutual obliteration. The " understanding heart," discerning good and bad, will seek to be informed, to be alert, to support every genuine effort to eliminate, or mitigate, the evils that stain our world, and constantly to draw support and strength from the God who knows how "to give good gifts unto his children." There is a cost then attached to this gift of the understanding heart. Perhaps that is why we don't always really want it. We can get along more comfortably without it. We forget the greater cost attached to our neglect. For the less we are aware of good and bad, the more adept we become at avoiding judgment, the less human we become. Who, in human history, has had the clearest insight into good and bad, the most absolute certainty that we must discern ? Surely the One who called Himself the " Son of Man "—because He is man as we ought to be. For Christian faith means little unless we seek union with Him. This is the purpose of our worship, of our prayers, our sermons, and our sacraments. And to be united with Him, St. Paul tells us, is to have " the mind of Christ." What He does is to sharpen our understanding, to educate our conscience, so that we may be awake to the world we live in, and penetrate beneath the surface judgments, the easy acquiescence, to the real struggle of good and bad in the affairs of men. When God gives the understanding heart we may be less comfortable but we are more alive. And there is room for live Christians not only in our churches but in public life to-day.

2. This call to moral judgment, to discerning good and bad, may sound to some like an invitation to pass sentence on our fellow-men, to classify our contemporaries into the " goodies " and " baddies " of a traditional Western. It is nothing of this kind. To discriminate between good and bad is not to be our neighbour's judge, or to divide all our fellows into sheep and goats. Only God can do that. (Have we forgotten

that Jesus says He *does* ?) We are to judge principles,
not people—not *who* is right but *what*. If our minds
have to be alert to good and bad, our hearts have also
to be open to understand. This is the other meaning
of the gift that we are seeking. An " understanding
heart " means not only discerning good and bad ; it
means also the sympathetic response to the needs,
the difficulties, the desires of others.

Have you ever noticed how the men and women you
know who are most sensitive to good and bad are
nearly always also the ones who understand best the
weaknesses and follies of individuals ? There are, of
course, some rigid persons of lofty principle, whose
obsession with good and bad makes them harsh and
unsympathetic. But the truly " understanding mind "
is also the " understanding heart." To be really
sensitive to good and bad is to sympathize with all
who are caught up in the struggle.

Look again at the Son of Man. No one has spoken
so bluntly about good and bad. " Every good tree
bringeth forth good fruit." And yet He sought out the
company of those who were classified among the bad of
His day—the publicans, the vagabonds, the prostitutes,
the excommunicate—and how He understood! Never
for a moment does He suggest that good and bad don't
matter. Never for a moment does He minimize God's
call for an absolute goodness. But in Him this goodness of God reached down to understand, to forgive, to
lift up. In that tremendous scene where He is left
alone with the woman taken in adultery—and all her
accusers had slunk away to think again about where
they stood in the matter of good and bad—how perfectly His understanding mind, His perception of right
and wrong, is blended with His understanding heart

" Woman, where are those thine accusers ? hath no man condemned thee ? " " No man, Lord." " Neither do I condemn thee : go, and sin no more."

Here then is the gift above all others, the gift that lifts life on to a different plane : the mind and heart that discerns good and bad and reaches out in love to understand. Jesus knows we need this gift supremely for He is aware of our perpetual closing in upon ourselves. " The ground of a certain rich man brought forth plentifully, and he thought within himself, saying, What shall I do ? " Here is the moment of decision we all know. What shall I do ? This was the moment for the understanding heart, for that man to have a good look at the world he lived in, and the conflict of good and bad. This was the moment to remember the men and women around him and use his time, his sympathy, and his goods to help them. What shall I do ? " And he said, This will I do : I will pull down my barns, and build greater ; and there will I bestow all my fruits and my goods. And I will say to my soul, Soul, thou hast much goods laid up for many years ; take thine ease, eat, drink, and be merry. But God said unto him, Thou fool . . ." This is the choice. To shut ourselves up in our own concerns, our own plans, our own ambitions—or to seek the understanding mind and heart, the mind that is sensitive to the conflict between good and bad, the heart that is sensitive to the needs of others. " Give therefore thy servant an understanding heart ! " The God who sent His Son to understand and to deliver, the God who responds to every slightest movement of our minds and hearts towards Him, will hear and respond. For this is a prayer that is always answered.

VII

THE LOGIC OF CHRISTIAN COMMITMENT

" And he said to them all, If any man will come after me, let him deny himself, and take up his cross daily, and follow me. For whosoever will save his life shall lose it : but whosoever will lose his life for my sake, the same shall save it."—LUKE IX. 23, 24.

SOME years ago I found myself reading through Gibbon's *Decline and Fall of the Roman Empire*. And one day I came across a very typical sentence in which he describes the national response to the religions of the day. I noted it down at the time and the other day it came back to my mind in the course of a discussion about religion in modern America. " The various modes of worship which prevailed in the Roman world," says Gibbon, " were all considered by the people as equally true ; by the philosophers as equally false, and by the magistrates as equally useful."

If Edward Gibbon were to visit this country to-day —listening to conversations, reading newspapers and magazines, watching television, attending churches, talking to ordinary folk, the intelligentsia, and men in authority—would his judgment be very different ?

" The various modes of worship . . . were considered by the people as equally true." Isn't this exactly the popular view to-day ? Protestant, Roman Catholic, Jewish, Christian Science, Mormon, Jehovah's Witnesses, Unitarian, Pentecostal, Bahai, Greek Orthodox,

Ethical Culture—every type of religion and of worship is generally considered as equally true. It doesn't matter if some of these faiths are almost diametrically opposed in their fundamental teachings, and have totally different conceptions of worship ; it is fashionable to insist that they are all equally true and right and good. To deny this is to be labelled intolerant and a religious bigot. The common phrase is : " We're all going the same way in the end and it doesn't matter how we get there." It is interesting to note that no one uses this argument in politics. You don't hear people saying that Communism and Western democracy are equally true and just different ways of arriving at the same end. It is only over our religious beliefs that this blanket is comfortably laid.

" The various modes of worship . . . were considered by the philosophers as equally false." Well, what about our intellectuals ? You don't have to move far in academic circles, or into the world of high-brow reviews, to discover an exact parallel to the situation described by Gibbon. The religions vaguely accepted by the common man as " equally true " are by and large discussed by the intellectual as " equally false." This is not so true to-day as it was thirty years ago, but the current trend towards popular religion is already provoking a cynical reaction. The ranks of the professional debunkers of popular piety are being reinforced by a number of serious men and women who find themselves unable to believe that any of the competing religions can possibly be true, and more and more inclined to interpret popular religion as an emotional release.

And what about Gibbon's " magistrates," who considered the " various modes of worship . . . equally

useful ? "   In every age the " powers that be " have
tended to use religion for their own ends.   In Army
language it is " good for the morale of the troops."
To-day, throughout the Western world, it is common
to hear religion spoken of in precisely this way.   It is
useful in preserving law and order, reducing crime and
delinquency, or as a bulwark against Communism.
All this is perfectly true of the major religions of the
day, and we have no right to impugn the sincerity of
any friends of religion in the field of government and
administration.   But we are in grave danger of forgetting that the first question about any religion is not
whether or not it is useful, but whether or not it is *true*.

" Equally   true,"   said   the   unthinking people ;
" equally   false,"   said   the   sceptical   philosophers ;
" equally useful," said the cynical magistrates.   And
into that happy equilibrium there erupted a force that
rocked the pedestals of them all—a force that shook the
Roman Empire to its foundations, and even disturbed
the equanimity of its historian.   That force was the
story of a crucified Galilean who was claimed to be the
living Lord of all mankind.   The story came on the lips
of wandering preachers, merchants, soldiers, com-
mercial   travellers,   slaves,   housewives,   officials — a
cross-section of the Empire.   And everywhere they
formed a community, a group that tied the most
divergent types together, and worked like a ferment in
society.   The one unifying, directing, sustaining power
behind this movement was a common faith in Christ
as the Lord and Saviour of the world.
    Another religion ?   Yes, but here at last was one that
Roman society could not absorb.   For this Church
would not set its Christ in the popular pantheon where

all religion was regarded as equally true. And this Church took its Gospel into the schools of the philosophers and dared them to prove it false. And when the magistrates debated whether to tolerate them as useful, or persecute them as subversive, the Christians displayed a heroic indifference ; calmly proclaiming that Christ was Lord whether they were elevated to power, or burned as living torches in Nero's Gardens.

The vitality of the Church in every age has always depended on this commitment to a Christ who will not be lined up with other lords as equally true ; who will not be dismissed as false by any passing philosophy, and who will never be a mere tool in the hands of government. Such commitment is a disturbing force in any society that likes to take its religion in innocuous doses, and to conceal behind a banner of tolerance a profound indifference to the truth.

This does not mean that to be Christians we must condemn all other religions and consign their adherents to hell. Still less does it mean that any one modern denomination contains the truth, the whole truth, and nothing but the truth. But it does mean that we recognize that Jesus Christ makes a unique claim upon our lives ; that we have to make up our minds about that claim. On the lower slopes of the divine hill there is much common ground among all religions. As we go higher the common ground is among the greater world religions. But as we go higher yet the paths diverge and every serious man or woman must make a choice. The figure of Jesus Christ looms out from the very presence of God and we hear His voice saying, " Come unto me ; I am the way, the truth, and the life." A Christian is one who says " Yes "—whether boldly and confidently, or slowly and timidly—and with that " Yes " he rejects the view that other faiths are equally true ; he is beyond the reach of the philosophers with their sceptical rejection ; and he is in the presence of a Lord who will not be " used " by any power on earth.

" If any man will come after me, let him deny himself, and take up his cross daily, and follow me." Looking at the Gospels again I have been struck by the insistent note of challenge on the lips of Jesus. It would be hard to construct from the Gospels the picture of a quiet teacher of religion and moral truth, taking His place in the line with others who have influenced men's minds. The narrative is studded with imperatives— " Come ! " " Believe ! " " Receive ! " " Seek ! "— and with questions that cut deep and demand an answer : " Who do *you* say that I am ? " " How is it you have no faith ? " " Do you love me ? " This is the Jesus, and no other, of whom the records tell us, and to-day He walks from the pages of this book, alive in the work and worship, the communion and sacraments of His Church, making this same call to total commitment. It was in this sense that He said, " I am come to send fire on the earth . . . I came not to send peace, but a sword."

What is the logic of this commitment ? What are we to say to our friends who find it hard to believe that anyone who lived two thousand years ago should be able to exert such a claim on us all, and who protest that they cannot make over their lives to any other than themselves ? And are we ourselves convinced that such Christian experience as we have rests on something more solid than a tradition we have accepted and on emotion that has fitfully been ours ? Do we not secretly want some such dramatic confirmation of our faith as Elijah got when the fire fell from heaven in answer to his prayer ?

The logic of Christian commitment is different from that of Mount Carmel when Elijah demanded : " Choose ye this day whom ye will serve." Jesus specifically rejected the temptation of the compelling, spectacular miracle—such as floating down to earth unharmed from the pinnacle of the Temple. But He gives us His own logic of commitment ; and it is found in words five times repeated in the Gospels : " If any man will come after me, let him deny himself, and take up his cross daily, and follow me." Why ? " For whosoever will save his life shall lose it ; but whosoever will lose his life for my sake, the same shall save it."

Jesus bases His claim on our commitment to a truth that is always valid—for the common people, the philosophers, and the magistrates of His day ; for the indifferent, the sceptical and the rulers of ours. It is the truth that we find our real selves by giving ourselves away. The self, the soul is not, and cannot be self-supporting, self-sufficient. Our personalities grow by contact with others. The journey we have all taken from infancy, through childhood and adolescence has been, or ought to have been, a process by which our self-hood has been discovered by giving ourselves away to others, adjusting our claims to theirs. The man who clings to his own inner centre, and seeks to save himself, is reverting to infancy ; the mature adult has learned to lose himself in that which is beyond himself. You will have noticed that the strong personalities are those who have most completely given themselves away, and not those who desperately try to hug and nurse their own selves and are for ever reading little booklets on how to develop poise and personality.

The fact is that our inner lives are made for commitment beyond ourselves. To hug them for ourselves, to claim the sole right of direction from the centre—is to lose our lives, to lose our souls. There is in religion too a kind of soul-saving that is the way to perdition. If our object in religion is simply the salvation of our own souls, if we are supremely concerned about our own inner security and peace, the soul itself will shrivel and die. " Whosoever will save his *soul*, his *life* (the word is the same) shall lose it."

This is the logic of commitment. We are made to find ourselves by losing ourselves, giving ourselves to that which is beyond us. In one way or another we have all done it. Those whom we love, those with whom we work, a cause in which we believe, an art to which we are dedicated—these are places in which by losing ourselves we really find ourselves. And the question that remains to be asked, the final link in the logic of commitment is : to what or to whom shall I commit my *entire* life ? Is there any power of overarching sublimity and truth in which I can confide the entire content of my life ? " In which ? " It cannot be a " which." No neuter power or principle can claim the commitment of a *person*. Is there a " whom "—a Supreme Person—a being whose nature responds to my trust and who has a right to my total devotion ?

This is where the Christ emerges from the heart of God with His total claim on our allegiance. " If any man will come after me, let him deny *himself*, and take up his cross daily, and follow me." Who is it that speaks ? Divine truth ? Yes, this is the deepest truth, the truth we discover in commitment. But He is more. He is the Lord who has Himself blazed the way for us in a body and a life like ours. He denied Himself. He gave Himself away. Virtue poured out of Him—over the needs and the sins and the sorrows of men and women. He gave Himself to the common people, to the philosophers, to the magistrates—until the day came when He literally took up His cross and on it lost His life. It is a living Lord who has passed that way who makes His claim upon us now. It is a claim based on the logic of our inner lives.

And have you noticed the simple logic of the act itself ? " If any man will come after me . . . let him follow me." It is almost a tautology. If you *will* follow, then follow. Nothing here of a cataclysm in our inner lives, no blinding flash of fire from heaven. Two steps—a No and a Yes. We deny ourselves, realize that our lives are not our own to do what we like with— No. And a Yes : Yes, Lord, I follow ; a Yes that has to be repeated *daily*, and a Yes that will involve the acceptance of whatever cross comes in our way, and there are many, of many different shapes and sizes. But, yes, with the cross, I follow.

That is all. And when we make that commitment we know that there is no other way that can be equally true, we know that this Christ conveys a wisdom beyond all philosophies, and we are in touch with a power beyond all earthly might.

" If any man will come after me, let him deny himself, and take up his cross daily, and follow me. For whosoever will save his life shall lose it : but whosoever will lose his life for my sake, the same shall save it."

VIII

OUR CHRISTIAN DUTY

" So likewise ye, when ye shall have done all those things which are commanded you, say, We are unprofitable servants : we have done that which was our duty to do."—LUKE XVII. 10.

THERE are two familiar hymns that begin with the words :

" Awake my soul, stretch every nerve,
And press with vigour on."

The other, even more famous, was written a century before by Bishop Ken, and it runs :

" Awake, my soul, and with the sun
Thy daily stage of duty run."

These are two contrasting moods, and each profoundly Christian. They both suggest a way of beginning the day, a kind of getting-up prayer as we roll out of bed and stretch our limbs. The one—" Awake, my soul, stretch every nerve, And press with vigour on "—is a kind of trumpet-call to action, a summons to the thrill and adventure of the Christian life. The other —designed perhaps for those who don't like trumpet-calls at 7.30 a.m.—contains a very plain reminder that the Christian life is also a matter of ordinary Christian duty. It is a sober, solemn and slightly uncomfortable hymn. And it has been omitted from our hymn-book.

This is worth thinking about. Have we got into the habit of romanticizing the Christian life, talking as if it consists entirely in crusades and campaigns, in miraculous interventions, in mystical moments, in comforts and consolations ? We would want to change the couplet :

" Awake, my soul, and with the sun
    Strive on until the world is won "

or

" Awake, my soul, and with the sun
    Let's have more light and health and fun."

That's the picture—excitement, energy, happiness, surprise—and we are quite right in believing that this is part of the Christian life. But it is not the whole of it, and we would do well to listen again to the old bishop :

" Awake, my soul, and with the sun
    Thy daily stage of duty run."

For in fact the Christian life is just as much a matter of " daily duty " as it is of comforts and thrills.

When I was a university chaplain I found difficulty in persuading students who had been captivated by the Christian Gospel that their service and witness were not uniquely in arranging meetings, promoting crusades and discussions, but also in the " daily stage of duty "—in other words, their studies. Every-one of us here is called to worship God not only in the high and holy moments when we are on our knees, or in church together, or carrying through a programme of evangelism, but in " the daily stage of duty "

whereby we earn our living, or look after a house.
Even in the work of the Church itself there is far
more " daily duty " in our calling than there is romance
and excitement. The thrill and impetus of a forward
movement would not be possible without the plodding,
faithful daily duty of members who devote weeks
to preparing files, checking lists, and making reports.
The Christian life is worked out at the typewriter, the
store-counter, the desk, and the kitchen sink as surely
as in our moments of inspiration and spiritual adventure.

This is why I want to think with you about our
Christian duty this morning. Like most preachers
I should prefer to speak of the more characteristic
Christian words—words like " grace " and " love "
and " faith " and " power." " Duty " has a dull
and moralistic sound, and it is not a specifically
Christian word at all. Yet there it is in the Bible :
the Old Testament is summed up in the words—
" Let us hear the conclusion of the whole matter :
Fear God, and keep his commandments : for this
is *the whole duty of man*." And if we begin to say,
" Yes, that's the Old Testament : the New has
another message," then what do we make of the
words of our text, the words of Jesus : " So likewise
ye, when ye shall have done all those things which
are commanded you, say, We are unprofitable servants :
we have done that which was our duty to do ? "

What Jesus has to say about duty is so radical that
few of us have ever really taken it in, and He uses
as an illustration a story which is almost brutal in
its impact. Before we reach the heart of His teaching
and examine His story we might think for a while
about what duty means to us to-day.

First, we can't help noticing that this is not a
popular word. " Duty " refers literally to something
that we owe. It is an obligation laid upon us. We
can have a duty to ourselves (don't you sometimes
say : " I owe it to myself to do such and such " ?)
or a duty to other people (a man owes his parents
respect and care ; he owes his wife fidelity to his
marriage vows ; he owes his country a loyalty and
service) or a duty to God (if we admit this, we'll see
later what it implies). Now I believe that to-day
we face a situation where many people virtually
refuse to admit they owe anyone anything at all.
And therefore they recognize no duties. The popular
phrases of our day reflect this attitude : " I couldn't
care less," " Let George do it," " I didn't ask to be
born," " What's in it for me ? " " Include me out."
That these are not always just humorous protests
is shown by the books of petulant philosophy that
have begun to appear. Angry young men write plays
and essays on the theme, apparently, that the world
owes them something while they on the other hand
owe no one anything at all.

I hope it is not a sign of irritable middle-age to
suggest that we are in danger of breeding a creditor
race that never admits a debt to anyone or anything.
This is not an indictment of any particular age-group.
It concerns us all. We have so stressed the notion
of human rights—and it has still to be stressed where
our less privileged neighbours are concerned—that
we tend to forget that no one can claim rights who
does not admit to duties. If I claim the right to walk
in comfort, and unmolested, up Madison Avenue,
I must admit my duty to contribute to its upkeep
and policing. If we claim the rights of free citizens

of a democratic country we must recognize our duty to take at least the elementary interest in its government that is implied by voting in an election. If a child claims the right to an education at public expense, surely he should be taught the corresponding duty of service to the community. There can be no rights without corresponding duties. Yet how often do we hear of rights to-day, and how seldom of duties. That is not quite true : we are quite quick to think of the neglected duties of other people. This is our trouble—even as I speak we tend to think of other people's duties—not our own—and I have been in danger of exercising the right to criticize others for not fulfilling *their* duties.

There is, however, this basic question : Do we recognize that we are debtors ? Have we a duty in life ? If a generation were to arise who refused to admit that anything was owed by them, who acknowledged no duties, we should be approaching the end of our civilization. Such an attitude is more subversive than any purely political ideology, and more menacing than any external foe.

Second. There is, thank God, in this and other countries a strong group of men and women who acknowledge what they are, recognize their duties and strive to practise them. Many draw their inspiration from the great world religions : others from the ethical resources of mankind. The long and honourable line of plain duty-doers has held society together. We can all think now of someone, perhaps in humble circumstances, of whom the greatest tribute that could be paid is simply : He did his duty : She did her duty. It may be an old-fashioned phrase but it stands for a virtue we recognize to-day in

every walk of life. Lately, for instance, men and
women of all religions, and of none, have recognized
in the late Pope the image of a man who did his
duty. As a Protestant minister, rather than reflect
on the gulf that separates me from that for which the
Papacy stands, I would rather ask myself : Do I
do my duty, as God gives me to see it, as faithfully
as he did his ?

There are more exciting ways of thinking about our
Christian way of life, and there is definitely a *truer*
way, but we don't reach them by rejecting the thought
of duty. In fact, for anyone seeking the Christian
way, this is an excellent place to begin. Many of
us, when confused about our faith and perplexed
as to what we can believe, are tempted to hope for
some special revelation, some divine flash in which
all becomes clear. There is a lot to be said for the
advice of Thomas Carlyle on this point : " Do the
duty which lies nearest thee, which thou knowest to
be a duty ! Thy second duty will already have become clearer." There are some Christians who never
have what you might call mystical experience. They
have to be content to think in terms of duty and
obedience. We have to remember that our Lord
welcomed not only the extravagant devotion of a
woman who flung herself before Him to wash His
feet with tears and dry them with her hair, but also
the laconic Roman officer who saw it all as duty and
obedience. ". . . speak the word only, and my servant
shall be healed. For I also am a man set under
authority, having under me soldiers, and I say unto
one, Go, and he goeth ; and to another, Come, and
he cometh ; and to my servant, Do this, and he
doeth it."

It would do us all good to ask ourselves whether we are seeking the comforts and stimulus of the Christian faith without first fulfilling the plain duties we accepted as disciples of Christ. During World War II, I once picked up in Germany a leaflet dropped by the R.A.F. It looked exactly like a German bank-note, and on it was written " ' I promise that no enemy bomber will penetrate the defences of the Reich ' Signed : Herman Göring : Date : September 1939." Across the paper was stamped in large letters : NICHT GÜLTIG—" not valid." Confirmed members of the Church have made solemn promises to be diligent in its worship and support, and in their use of the means of Grace. As the years pass by, for how many must the words " not valid " be applied ? A simple recall to duty can often be the beginning of a recreation of living faith.

Is duty then the beginning and the end of our Christian life ? The answer is Yes—but only on condition that we expand the idea of duty to the tremendous dimensions that Jesus gives it. The trouble is that we can develop a duty-religion that falls far short of the Christian Gospel. You might call it the religion of limited liability. We decide that there are certain rules to be kept. We accept the Ten Commandments as our standard. We then divide our life into spheres of duty—duty to family, duty to business, duty to country, duty to God. In these spheres we delimit the area of the possible, and do our utmost to attain it. The result is a life of rectitude, sobriety and reliability—but also, it may be, of harshness, censoriousness, and pride.

Who was it that said " God, I thank thee, that I am

not as other men are, extortioners, unjust, adulterers. . . .
I fast twice in the week, I give tithes of all that I
possess "? The Pharisee in the Temple. And Jesus
said that the wretched publican who merely said :
" God be merciful to me, a sinner " went down to his
house " justified (accepted) rather than the other."

How can we fulfil our duty without developing the
lines of the Pharisee—the lines our Lord seems to
have detested most ? Only by letting Jesus expand
for us the idea of duty till we see what is really implied.

You see, the religion of limited liability keeps us
well in the range of what we can do. If our duty,
for instance, is not to commit murder, or theft, or
adultery, many can say with the rich young man
who talked with Jesus about eternal life : " All these
have I kept from my youth up." But when we allow
our Lord to explore and expand the real meaning of
the Commandments, when we hear Him say that to
be angry is the sin of murder, to covet is to steal, to
play with the idea is adultery, then we are not in
such a hurry to say : " All these have I kept from my
youth up."

The religion of limited liability means accepting
an area of duty that we know we can fulfil. This has
even on occasion had fair official sanction in the
Church where men speak of two levels of Christian
living—the approximate goodness of the ordinary
man and the total goodness of the saint. If we fall
for that we can easily say : " Sainthood is not for
me : I'll take a pass degree and leave the honours to
others." Then we can easily be satisfied with our
level of achievement, and with self-satisfaction goes
criticism of others, and the door is wide open to the
sins our Lord so violently condemned.

Now we are ready to hear what Jesus has to say about our Christian duty. " So likewise ye, when ye shall have done all those things which are commanded you, say, We are unprofitable servants : we have done that which was our duty to do." " *All those things* which are commanded you . . ." And what are they ? Not a list of simple propositions, but nothing less than the total programme of love to God and man as set out in His own life and teaching. I see no way in which we can modify the clear demands of the Gospel. Didn't He summarize His Sermon on the Mount with the words : " Be ye therefore perfect, even as your Father which is in heaven is perfect " ?

This is our Christian duty—and nothing less. How do you feel about it ? Does it seem so hopelessly impractical that we need never give it a moment's thought ? Or if we do think seriously about it, won't it tend to hang round our necks like the albatross in the *Ancient Mariner*—a dead weight of obligation loading our conscience forever ?

In fact this total obligation of the Christian—however back-breaking it looks—carries with it the secret of deepest satisfaction and ultimate joy. For out of its acceptance come the two qualities we desperately need—humility and hope.

To know that our Christian duty means loving God with all our heart, and soul, and mind, and strength, and our neighbours as ourselves, will deliver us from ever sitting back complacent that we have done our duty. It will prevent that feeling of self-congratulation with which we sometimes review our devotions or our unsuitable gifts. What a violent illustration Jesus uses just here. A farmer in first-century Palestine has a slave. (Jesus is not here concerned with whether this relationship was right or not—He's talking of what did happen.) Can you imagine, He says, that when the slave comes in from work that his master will fuss over him, saying, " My dear fellow, you must be tired ; what a lot of work you have done. Come right in and I'll get your supper for you " ? His hearers would laugh at the idea. " Right ", says Jesus. " So likewise ye, when ye shall have done all those things which are commanded you, say, We are unprofitable servants : we have done that which was our duty to do."

Our Christian duty is what we owe to God. We owe everything to God. Therefore there is no room for self-congratulation when we do a fraction of our duty. If that thought doesn't keep us humble, what can ? And when you look at the lives of the saints, the finest men and women we have known, you will find that such a humility is at the root of their goodness and their love. They literally do not expect praise. They are servants. They have just done their duty. Such an attitude—hard though it is for all of us, is at the root of a satisfying and literally carefree life. For it removes us from the territory of claim and counter-claim, pride, criticism and self-pity. When we see what it means to owe everything to God we realize the immensity of our debt and we are not hypocrites when we begin our worship together with a confession of our sins.

And with this humility comes hope. For such a duty would not be laid upon us unless God had seen in us the possibilities of spiritual growth beyond our wildest dreams. Is such a duty tolerable for mortal man ? The Son of God Himself comes to show us that it is. He lives our life, and the Sermon on the

I.A.P.—6

Mount comes alive before us. " But as many as received him, to them gave he power to become the sons of God." This is our hope. We are called to share that life. To settle for less, to set for ourselves lesser duties than we can fulfil, is to turn our back on the highest calling known to man, and to refuse the dynamic companionship of Christ.

" We are servants, we have done that which was our duty to do." If this is our attitude we are given entrance to the Kingdom where there is no end to our growth, a growth that needs not only this life but one beyond for its endless fulfilment. And when we are willing to admit that we owe everything to God, and that our plain duty stretches up beyond the limits of our highest achievement, then it is revealed to us that God calls us in the end not servants, but sons, and duty is translated into love.

IX

ADAM AND THE ASTRONAUT

" And God blessed them, and God said unto them, Be fruitful, and multiply, and replenish the earth, and subdue it : and have dominion over the fish of the sea, and over the fowl of the air, and over every living thing that moveth upon the earth."—GEN. I. 28.

SHORTLY after the first sputnik went into orbit and began to send back its " Beep-beep " message to the listening nations, a lady turned to me at a dinner-party and said : " You ministers can say what you like : somehow that thing has got between me and God."

I am sure this feeling that man's new adventure into space does something to our religious convictions is fairly widespread to-day. Pure belief in God the Father Almighty would be quite unaffected by any scientific discovery whatever, but none of us has such a pure belief. Our knowledge of God is wrapped up in a package containing all kinds of pictures and traditions and explosive emotions, any one of which may be seriously threatened by some scientific discovery. And it is very hard for us to disentangle the central core of our faith from the incidentals with which it has been wrapped up. Religion operates in all of us with a set of symbols and images that go far back into the racial memory of man. Science has its own set of symbols and images that change with a bewildering rapidity and are concerned with pushing out towards the future. It is inevitable that from time to time the advance of science produces a conflict of images, a clash of symbols. At such a moment Christians can either hug their religious package and shout defiance at the scientist, or else they can rediscover the living centre of their faith, the living God whose universe this is, and who has set man in it to explore its truth and exploit its riches, the God who is not only the God of the past but also of the future.

A hundred years ago Christian people were thrown into confusion, and even uproar, by the publication of Darwin's *Origin of Species*. The suggestion that the human race may physically share some common ancestor with the monkeys seemed for many people to threaten the inner core of their faith. We find it difficult now to see why. What was being touched was no more than a wrapping, but the wrapping was a symbol soaked in religious emotion. To-day whether we agree with Darwin or not depends on our scientific, not our religious judgment. Whether he was right or wrong (or, as seems to be generally agreed, partly right and partly wrong), is a question to be decided by continued research and investigation—not by shouting slogans and taking sides.

And now the monkeys have been at it again. Whether or not they preceded us down from the trees, they have certainly preceded us up into space.

> " In 1959 the mind
> Is somewhat paralysed to find
> The astronauts in Darwin's plan—
> First the monkey, then the man."

Seriously, of course the problem is totally different. The question raised by our little friends Able and Baker was not one of our ancestry but of our progeny. Is the human race going to take off in a new direction —a direction it was never meant to take? Are we on the verge of an era when human beings are going to transgress " the bounds of their habitation " and go soaring off to worlds unknown—and forbidden? (Will the integration problem for our descendants rage around " mixed marriages with the Martians " ?)

However wild our speculations may be, the sober truth is that much that used to be sheer fantasy has now become scientific possibility. And it is not surprising that religious questions are beginning to stir. Is this a new Tower of Babel that we are beginning to construct—an attempt to " build us a city and a tower, whose top may reach unto heaven "—so that " we shall be as gods " ? And, if indeed there are other inhabited worlds, what does that do to our thoughts of God and man, and the coming of Christ to this earth at that particular time and place? Has the Bible any kind of validity in this new and startling environment? If we don't ask these questions, be sure our children will.

Where do we begin? Not with the astronauts but with Adam—the Bible name for Man. It is Man we are concerned with, the root Man, the Old Adam —the kind of creature we are. He is the one who is engaged in these discoveries. The majestic mysteries of the heavens dazzle our minds, but they are not really as astounding as the eyes behind the telescope and the brain behind the eyes. Every discovery that seems to diminish man's stature in the universe at the same time augments his astonishing control. From the Stone Age to the Romans, from Galileo to Darwin, from Einstein to the present moment the real question is the nature and destiny of man. And, in the space age as much as in any other, this is fundamentally a religious question. Science can tell us the story of man's ancestry. Science can penetrate into the secrets of nature. Science can show us how things work. But the scientific method is not concerned with who man really is, why he exists at all, or what he is meant to do. Science can show us how to get into outer space, but it is not science that decides whether we ought to, and what to do when we get there.

When we understand this distinction we are ready to hear what religion, and in particular the Christian faith, has to say about Adam—the nature of man.

"And God blessed them, and God said unto them, Be fruitful, and multiply, and replenish the earth, and subdue it : and have dominion over the fish of the sea, and over the fowl of the air, and over every living thing that moveth upon the earth." This is the language of religious faith, not of the laboratory, or anthropological research. That doesn't make it less important, but more. For every action of man, that will affect us all for good or evil, depends in the end on what is believed about who man is. Four men are now meeting at Geneva. Each of the four has at his disposal the instruments of modern science. Each represents a country possessing material power far in excess of anything yet seen on earth. Yet we know that this power is impotent to solve the major problems of the world—unless it is harnessed to a faith, a faith in the nature and destiny of man. Who is Adam ? and what is he meant to do, and to become ?

The Bible answer is as clear and relevant to-day as it has ever been. " And *God* blessed them, and *God* said . . ." Man is not an accident, a freak of nature. Man is not an independent being with no responsibilities. He is designed by God, and he is responsible to God. That essential Adam, who has endured from the first recognizable human to the most brilliant thinker of to-day, has stamped upon him the claim of his Creator. Adam is God's man. His true nature is seen in his kinship with the good and holy God. And his destiny—his chief end—is " to glorify God and enjoy him for ever." " And *God* blessed them, and *God* said . . ." This is the real Adam. He is called into being by the Word of God, and through the centuries, sometimes dimly, sometimes most vividly, he has known that " man shall not live by bread alone, but by every word that proceedeth out of the mouth of God."

Now notice what follows : " And God blessed them, and God said unto them, Be fruitful, and multiply, and replenish the earth, and subdue it : and have dominion over the fish of the sea, and over the fowl of the air, and over every living thing that moveth upon the earth." Under God man is given a position of astounding freedom and power. There is implanted in Adam the dynamic of procreation, and the promise of mastery over nature and the animal kingdom. Once you have heard the opening words—" God said " —you find here a charter of confidence and freedom, a declaration of independence, a legacy of infinite wealth. This is what man is truly meant to be—a creature, born of the dust of the earth, but fashioned in the image of God. You have seen how the sun, shining down on a busy city at noon and giving light to all, finds just here and there a point of bright reflection. So the Spirit of the living God, brooding over the dark mysteries of creation, sustaining all things in being, finds in man alone the answering glint of understanding, power, and love.

This understanding of ourselves as called under God to a self-confidence and hope, to an increasing mastery of nature, and to a destiny beyond the limits of the material and the animal, is sadly lacking in our thinking of to-day. Adam has been down-graded. We live under the shadow of the suggestion that, after all, man is really part of nature, an end-product of an undirected, meaningless process of evolution, doomed to eventual extinction in the cold silences of space. Or we are told that man is the victim of an impersonal logic of history, a dialectic materialism that drives him like a robot to the ant-heap society. As never before despair has humanity by the throat, and our books, our plays, our pictures, and our music reflect the disorder, the sense of futility, and the moral chaos of our age. It is a paradox that at the very moment when Adam's dominion over nature has reached unparalleled dimensions his self-confidence is evaporating and he is ready to let nature win. Of what use is it to reach for the stars, if we believe that man is no more than a grain of star-dust ? Of what use is it to control the animal world if we believe that man is no more than an animal himself ?

Even religious people have been infected with this loss of nerve. Hence these timid questions about man's right to new fields of knowledge. Hence these

fears about the new dimensions we are about to enter
—as if somehow they belonged to another, unknown
God. " Whither shall I go from thy spirit ? or whither
shall I flee from thy presence ? " In the gently
humming cabin of his nose-cone the astronaut is still
the same Adam called by the same God to the adventure
of discovery and dominion.

For the Christian there is only one cause for fear.
And it doesn't lie in the daring discoveries of man,
in any inexorable laws of nature or human nature,
or in some vague threat in outer space. Jesus spoke
with utter confidence about our relationship to the
world around us, visible and invisible. It is the
Father's house with many mansions to which He offers
us the key. Every least creature is the object of
God's care and nothing happens that is beyond the
circle of His love. " Not a sparrow—or a nose-cone
—falls to the ground without your Father." " *Fear
not*, therefore : ye are of more value than many
sparrows." There was only one fear He recognized
—the fear of hell. And what is hell ? Not some
arbitrary punishment reserved for eternity, but separation from God. Hell is man without God ; deliberately
shutting himself off from God. It is the result of man
claiming the creation and defying the Creator, seizing
the dominion and forgetting who conferred it. " And
God said . . . have dominion." Hell begins with the
serpent's whisper : " Yea, *hath* God said ? "
The dignity of man comes with his call to stride
confidently into the unknown, " a little lower than
the angels . . . crowned with glory and honour." The
tragedy of man comes with his rejection of the God
who made him. And the Old Adam, as we know, is

this God-rejecting nature of ours. So it would often appear as though religion merely added to the sum of pessimism about mankind. What is the use of telling the story of this ideal Adam summoned to a glorious destiny, if all we have is the Old Adam, this rebellious nature, driving mankind to destruction ?

It is not all we have. We have Christ. The Christian view of man is not just founded on a verse in Genesis describing man as God meant him to be. Nor is it founded on the malediction of man adrift from God, the fallen Adam. It is founded on the One who came to reveal who man is and restore us to the Father— the " Son of man who came to seek and to save that which was lost."

> " O loving wisdom of our God !
> When all was sin and shame,
> A second Adam to the fight
> And to the rescue came."

These lines from Newman's great hymn, " Praise to the holiest in the height," are inspired by the New Testament thought of Christ as the " Second Adam," the One in whom and by whom the great promise of Genesis can be fulfilled. " And God blessed them, and God said unto them, Be fruitful, and multiply, and replenish the earth, and subdue it : and have dominion over the fish of the sea, and over the fowl of the air, and over every living thing that moveth upon the earth." The throbbing confidence and potential of man standing ever on the threshold of new discovery can be restored by Him, and by Him alone, who has actually walked on this solid earth of ours and now lives victorious in the heart of God. " For as in Adam all die, so in Christ shall all be made alive."

The Christian, then, has one sure centre for his thoughts about the destiny of man.   In the presence of Christ he sees the image of God restored and hears again the summons to the adventure of the sons of God.   He is not afraid of the future, for Christ is the way.   He is not afraid of any discovery of science, for Christ is the truth.   He is not afraid of death, for Christ is the life.   Above all he is delivered from that one true fear of separation from God, for he knows that " neither death, nor life, nor angels, nor princi-palities, nor powers, . . . nor things to come, nor height, nor depth, nor any other creature—sputniks or visitors from outer space—shall be able to separate us from the love of God, which is in Christ Jesus our Lord."

This is not always true for you and me.   I said it was true in the presence of Christ.   And that is where we are now, and where we should ever be.

X

SAINTS IN HIDING

" Now when they beheld the boldness of Peter and John, and had perceived that they were unlearned and ignorant men, they marvelled ; and they took knowledge of them, that they had been with Jesus."—ACTS IV. 13 (R.V.).

SOME years ago two men were travelling in a train in England. One of them stared for a long time at another passenger ; then turned to his friend and said : " I bet you half a crown that's the Archbishop of Canterbury." " I'll take you," said the other. " I don't believe it is." So the first went over to the stranger and said : " Excuse me, but aren't you the Archbishop of Canterbury ? " The gentleman addressed laid down his paper, glared at him, and said : " You get to blazes out of here and mind your own —— business ! " Whereupon the other returned to his friend saying, " The bet's off. We still don't know if he's the Archbishop or not."

That story raises for us a much more important question than that of recognizing an Archbishop. How, in fact, do you recognize a Christian ? Perhaps you might say that the outburst of the stranger in the train proved not only that he was not the Archbishop, but also that he was not even a Christian. But we couldn't say even that for certain. He may have been a convinced church-member having—as

we all do—an off-day. In any case we can't just
apply a negative rule. All people who refrain from
being rude on trains are not necessarily Christians.
Is there any way in our everyday life by which we
can recognize a Christian man or woman ?

Suppose you were an artist commissioned to design
one of those big posters encouraging people to come
to church. You have to create an image of the Christian
family heading for church on a Sunday morning.
Probably in the end you would come up with one of
those pink, smiling, middle-income couples with two
gleaming children. It would be difficult to do anything else. Yet you know very well that vast numbers
of active, worshipping Christians have not the slightest
resemblance to this happy family—who look sus-
piciously like the same group whom we have seen
gathered joyfully round the latest refrigerator, or
eagerly scrubbing their spotless teeth. The fact is
that you could draw any kind of human being you
like to think of—old or young, beautiful or ugly,
rich or poor, white or black or brown, healthy or sick,
married or unmarried, gay or serious—and you could
still have a Christian as we know him in the world
to-day. There is no outward sign by which you can
at once recognize a Christian. To draw the portrait
of a Christian is as hard as to attempt to delineate the
features of our Lord Himself. Every artist imparts
to the lineaments of Jesus something of the spirit of
his own age, and we have the Christs of the ancient
world—Roman Christs, Byzantine Christs, medieval
Christs, Victorian Christs, and Christs with the features
of the African, the Indian, the Eskimo, and the
Japanese. Every man is reflected in His face ; and
the face of His followers is the face of every man and

every woman. The universal Christ draws all men to Himself.

You cannot, therefore, recognize a Christian by his outward shape. Has it then to do with the contours of his mind, the way he thinks? We know something of the impact of the Gospel on the mind of man, the mark that Christ has made on the intellectual development of mankind, and the challenge to us all to think through the implication of our faith. But it cannot be claimed that you can recognize a Christian by the intrinsic superiority of his mind. It is not brain-power that makes a man or woman a recognizable Christian. In our text we read that the authorities who had Peter and John arrested considered them " unlearned and ignorant men." The Revised Standard Version is slightly more accurate in translating " uneducated, common men." That is what they were, these apostles. Peter and John did not have the intellectual training of their enemies, or of their future colleague, Paul. Jesus did not say : " Come unto me all ye with I.Q. over 100," and there has never been a period in Christian history when the mind alone was the criterion of discipleship.

It's not the outward appearance ; it's not the mental ability ; nor is it cultural interests or even moral passion that make us recognize a Christian. A man or woman can be a great artist without being a Christian, and some of the most fervent moral crusaders of our day completely reject the Christian creed. By what sign, then, can a Christian be recognized? It almost looks as if we had exhausted the possibilities.

Could it be that there is a sense in which a Christian is not meant to be recognized? Perhaps it's just that we have to-day a passion for recognition. We like to bundle people into groups and tie labels on them for all to read. We are happier when we can categorize our neighbours and drop them into appropriate slots in our minds. It saves us the trouble of really trying to understand them. This is a day of badges, and pledges, and affiliations. It would simplify matters if there were some way of becoming a registered Christian. And so, of course, there is. Church membership involves public recognition that we are Christians. But church members do not, as yet, wear badges on their breasts to proclaim their faith. They blend with the population, unmarked and undistinguished. Should it be otherwise?

I had a day-dream when preparing this sermon. There was a huge hotel teeming with delegates to a Christian convention. The lobbies were laced with streams of people wearing huge coloured labels— " Orthodox," " Roman Catholic," " Episcopal," " Baptist," " Methodist," " Presbyterian," or just " Christian." In the banquet-room a wall-to-wall diagram listed the major problems of the world and the appropriate committees for dealing with them. Banners hung from the roof, and slogans flashed from every corner. Through the great room and down the stairs came One without a badge. He passed through the vociferous groups in the vestibule and out through a side-door into the street. No one knew Him as He walked among the crowds, but as He passed something seemed to happen to those tense and anxious faces, to those eager hurrying steps, to those puzzled and bewildered eyes. He was the only one who stopped when a woman stumbled and fell on the sidewalk, but when He had helped her up there were others now

ready to assist. Then He went on His way unrecognized—and His face was the face of Christ.

" Ye are the salt of the earth," said Jesus. I
know when I am eating a dish that is properly salted
—or, at least, I should at once if it were not. But
the salt is invisible. That other unsalted dish looks
exactly the same. And my hostess has not stuck
on a label reading : " This dish is properly salted."

The strongest Christian influence in our world has
always been that of the unrecognized—the saints
in hiding. These are the people who need no badge.
The distinguishing mark upon them is one that they
cannot help and of which they are unaware. It is
the simple contagion of Christ, the reflection of His
spirit, the presence of His grace. In the words of
our text they have " been with Jesus."

This is the definition of a saint. The word has
come to have a semi-official sound as it is conferred
on certain men and women in Christian history.
Or it has taken on a miserable, perverted connota-
tion as in the word " sanctimonious." Or we use
it seriously to describe the very finest Christian that
we know. In the New Testament it is simply the
name given to those who have " been with Jesus "—
ordinary men and women, who, with all their faults
and follies, have made contact with the living Christ,
and been united with Him.

According to the New Testament we are all " called
to be saints." And this is a work that goes on in
the silent depths of our being. When, in one way or
another, we have yielded ourselves to Christ, deep
within us there is a saint in hiding. There is no
outward and indelible sign of His existence. The
water of baptism dries off upon our brow, but the

grace of the Lord Jesus Christ, and the love of God, and the communion of the Holy Spirit, are at work in our heart.

How often Jesus speaks of the hidden, invisible powers of the Kingdom He proclaims. Salt—it gives the flavour, it preserves from corruption, but you don't see it. Leaven working hidden in the dough; light that reveals the beauty of the world but is never itself the object of our attention; the microscopic seed that sends through the dark damp earth the radiant power that breaks out in the foliage of spring. When you pray, go away and close the door and talk to your Father in secret. When you give, don't give your cheques an escort of sounding sirens. When you give something up for the sake of the Kingdom, act as though you hadn't. Again and again we are warned that it is not the outward sign which makes a Christian. Jesus dismisses all such claims for public recognition with the devastating words : " They have their reward." What matters is the real bent and direction of our lives in that secret place known only to us and to the God " unto whom all hearts are open, all desires known, and from whom no secrets are hid." If then it can be said that we " have been with Jesus," have listened to His claim, have bowed before His majesty, have been touched by His cross, have known something of the triumph of His love, then there is within us a saint in hiding, and it is not our business how or when he may be recognized.

It is even dangerous for us to think of him at all. I mean that the moment we become self-conscious about our Christian faith it begins to wither. Go looking for the saint in you—and he disappears. There is a vivid picture of this process in the Gospel.

I.A.P.—7

Jesus calls to Peter to come to Him across some stormy
water. So long as his eyes are on the Master he goes
straight ahead. Then he begins to think about himself : What am I doing ? Look at me, Peter, walking
on the water ! And it's rough, it's deep—help, Lord,
I'm sinking ! In the Christian life the advice given
to those who walk in dangerous places holds good :
Don't look down ! " Let us run with patience the
race that is set before us, looking unto Jesus the author
and finisher of our faith." He will take care of that
saint within.

The mark of a Christian, then, is our genuine devotion to our Lord in the hidden centre of our lives.
It is the test of solitude. When no one is there to
watch, when no pressures are on us from outside,
when no one hears what we say, are we then " with
Jesus "—accepting His way, seeking His strength,
wanting His will ? But we shall be wrong if we
imagine that this means that our faith can be hidden,
that Christian influence is unmarked and unnoticed
in our world, that there is no point at which we must
as Christians stand up and be counted. There is a
temptation for us to-day when world affairs are so
complex and disheartening, when controversial decisions are demanded of us, when Christian councils
and conferences thicken on the ground, to withdraw
from the arena, to cultivate our own spiritual garden.
" To be with Jesus " can then become a retreat from
responsibility, a soft and selfish refuge from the storm.
In fact the real test of whether we have truly
" been with Jesus " is the whole-heartedness of our
engagement in the world. Whether we like it or
not there comes a moment and a place where our

commitment must be recognized—not as a tribute to our virtue, but as a sign of where we stand and whose we are. " Let your light so shine before men, that they may see your good works . . ." and say " what a saint that person is "? No—" and glorify your Father which is in heaven." This is the inevitable result of a true devotion to Christ. " A city set on a hill cannot be hid."

What do we read about Peter and John in the presence of a hostile crowd ? " They took knowledge of them, that they had been with Jesus." They recognized this one thing in them—not their power, their prestige, their appearance or their brain : simply that " they had been with Jesus." But they re-cognized it. This is a recognition that we do not seek. It is not self-conscious ; but it is inevitable. From the day when Jesus hung upon a cross, from the day when His first disciples told the world He had risen from the dead, men and women have recognized Him and those who have been with Him. They cannot help it. For there is no stronger power to change a human life, to cleanse a nation, to deliver the world from evil, than this collective witness of the saints.

When fear and bewilderment are abroad, when men and women sense behind the revelry of the moment a writing on the wall they cannot under-stand, they will turn, as in the days of Belshazzar, to the astrologers and soothsayers and the wise men of the day. But when these have been heard they will hear again the words of the Queen of Persia : " There is a man in thy kingdom in whom is the spirit of the holy gods." In all ages the instinct of men has been at such moments to seek those who have " the spirit of the holy." In ancient Persia

they found such a man in Daniel, the young Jew of
whom we read that in the dissolute court of the day
" he purposed in his heart that he would not defile
himself."

The Church of Jesus Christ is called to be such
an instrument in our world to-day. And the Church
of Jesus Christ is composed of those who, in one way
or another, have " been with Jesus." That is how
we are to be recognized, not by any outward badge,
but by the compulsive infection of the saint in hiding.
When we think of the work we go to do to-morrow,
the conversations we shall have with friends, our
comments on the issues of the day, our behaviour
in our homes, we must now in our worship be led to
pray, without affectation or pretence :

> " O that it might be said of me,
>   Surely thy speech betrayeth thee ;
>   Thou wast with Jesus of Galilee."

XI

FAITH WITHOUT CRUTCHES

" How shall we sing the Lord's song in a strange land ? "—
PS. CXXXVII. 4.

WHAT we hear in the Bible is not only the voice
of God calling us to repent and believe. We
hear from time to time the sound of man answering
back. I am not thinking now of the submissive or
the joyful answer, but of the growling and grumbling
of the Israelites in the wilderness, the fiery impatience
of Saul, the sulking of Jonah, the lamentations of
Jeremiah, and the courageous self-vindication of Job.
In these we hear an echo of our own deep questionings
of God's ways—Why should this happen to me ?
How can I believe in God *now* ? Where is the justice
in His world ? What kind of faith can I have in
His love ?

It was this kind of protest that rose like a mist
from " the waters of Babylon." We have to imagine
a group of displaced persons, the victims of defeat
and mass-transportation from Jerusalem to Babylon,
huddled together beside the banks of this mighty
foreign river—so utterly different from the little
stream of the Jordan. They are sunk in a communal
nostalgic misery—that mood of listless despair and
infectious gloom that the French call *le cafard* and
others have known as " barbed-wire-sickness." It

93

is the Sabbath, but the musical instruments hang on the trees unused, and no one has the spirit to strike up one of the Songs of David.

Then a group of Babylonian soldiers come swaggering past—out on leave and looking for some fun. " Look ! " says one of them, " a bunch of miserable Hebrews. Let's make them sing us one of their native songs." And in a moment the wretched exiles are surrounded by an uproarious group of soldiers, jeering and laughing and prodding them with their spears, till some thin wail of melody is forced from their lips.

" By the rivers of Babylon, there we sat down, yea, we wept, when we remembered Zion. We hanged our harps upon the willows in the midst thereof. For there they that carried us away captive required of us a song ; and they that wasted us required of us mirth, saying, Sing us one of the songs of Zion. How shall we sing the Lord's song in a strange land ? "

One Sunday evening as a student in Edinburgh I heard a vivid description of this incident in the course of an arresting sermon by Dr. James S. Stewart. Little did I imagine that a few years later the scene would come to life again for me. It happened in this way : In the early days of World War II, a rather foolish and uninspired song was plugged right across the British Isles. Its chorus was " We're going to hang out our washing on the Siegfried Line." Some months later a weary column of British prisoners-of-war was being force-marched across Europe past that same Siegfried Line ; and one day a group of them was surrounded by some young Nazi troops who demanded at the point of the bayonet that they sing this song. Fun for them—and added misery for the prisoners. It was the Psalm alive again, just as, five years later, another psalm perfectly expressed a different mood : " When the Lord turned again the captivity of Zion, we were like them that dream!"

The real question behind the lament—" How shall we sing the Lord's song in a strange land ? "—is not whether we feel like singing patriotic songs in moments of gloom, but whether we have a faith that can travel. Is the " Lord's Song " in our hearts so completely geographically conditioned that it dies away the moment an environment changes ? The Hebrew religion had been so rooted in Jerusalem, their sacrificial ritual so exclusively dependent on the Temple, that the disaster and destruction that laid them both in ruins, left most of the exiles in utter despair. Their religion was no longer a living faith, but a sad and tenacious memory. " If I forget thee, O Jerusalem, let my right hand forget her cunning."

We do not always realize the influence of environment on our religious convictions. Most of us had our first glimpse of God, our first flicker of response to the Christian Gospel, within the circle of our parents' home and local church. Others associate their faith with some person, some movement, some group experience at a later stage in life. One way or another we have all some environmental crutch on which our faith has leaned. This is as it should be, for " no man is an island " and faith, like everything else, is mediated to us along the continental highways of our common life. We need the local reference, the familiar atmosphere, the comfortable presence.

But just how much do we need them ? That we only discover when they are taken away, and we find

ourselves in a strange land. A boy is brought up in a
small community in the Middle West, where his
family are devoted Christians, and the local church
is the centre of their social life. In this atmosphere he
is baptized, confirmed, and becomes active in the choir
and all the youth activities. Suddenly in his early
twenties he finds himself in his first job—in the city
of New York. The entire environment has changed.
Few of his contemporaries are at all interested in the
Protestant Church ; no one knows—or cares—whether
he attends worship or not. As he stands among the
twinkling lights and lurid posters of Times Square,
the choir of Second Presbyterian, Doakesville, seems
very far away. " How shall we sing the Lord's song
in a strange land ? "

A woman lives for sixty years in a relatively sheltered environment. Her faith is nurtured in a con-
ventional home and church, so that her religion is an
integral part of the secure and well-ordered background
of her life. She has had good parents, a good marriage,
and sufficient comforts and interests to keep her relatively happy and content. Suddenly, without warning,
disaster strikes. It may be accident, illness, bereave-
ment, or a financial blizzard—or a terrible combination
of them all. In a moment her entire environment has
changed. The home, the street, the shops, the church
may still be there—but she is in a strange land, as
surely exiled from the life she knew as if she had been
transported to another planet. And her faith ? " How
shall we sing the Lord's song in a strange land ? "

A student—and we can be students at any age—
whose religion was absorbed in Sunday School and
subconsciously tied in with his childhood picture of
the universe, finds himself launched into an intensive

course of science, or philosophy. There comes a moment, almost unperceived, when he shakes loose from the patterns of thought in which he has been reared ; his ideas begin to soar, and soon, to his astonishment, he is living in a different world. And when some day he pulls out from the recesses of his mind the religious beliefs that used to satisfy him, they seem so thin, so childish that they are no longer adequate for the strange new land to which his mind has travelled. " How shall we sing the Lord's song in a strange land ? "

These are examples of what can happen when our faith is too narrowly localized, when our religion leans too heavily on the crutches of home, environment, or early training. Can your faith travel ? Just how heavily are you and I leaning on the crutches of our parents' faith, our church's faith, our childhood religion, or the comfort of our surroundings, or comparative smoothness of our way of life ? The season of Lent is designed to help us to travel out into the wilderness for a while—either in fact or by the use of a consecrated imagination—so that we can discover this faith of which the Gospel speaks, a faith that stands firm when the rains descend, and the floods come and the winds of adversity blow and beat upon the soul. For there *is* a faith that needs no crutches, a faith that can sing the Lord's song in the strange land. There was a song, you remember, that rose into the Jerusalem night when eleven men rose from a simple table and made their way to a garden called Gethsemane. It was a strange land, then, for Jesus. The city He loved was transformed into a bastion of evil ; the Temple where He had worshipped now glimmered in the moonlight as the shrine of His enemies ; the pulse of the people in their sleeping homes was now quickening with hatred and rejection ; and in the eyes of the friends around Him He read cowardice and fear. Yet it was the Lord's song upon His lips as He travelled that night through the strange land.

So it was a few years later when a Roman jailer was wakened in the night. Through the prison walls came the sound of singing. " At midnight Paul and Silas prayed, and sang praise unto God : and the prisoners heard them." These were the men who had broken loose from their ancestral faith, who had then left the new security of their local church and were emissaries of Christ in a pagan land. These were the men who that day had been given a Roman flogging and fastened in a cell with stocks on their legs. How—just how—were they able to " sing the Lord's song in a strange land " ?

There is no quick way to reach such a faith, and we shouldn't be in too much of a hurry to fling away the crutches of the past. But for those who have begun to understand that Christian faith is neither a matter of forcing ourselves to believe the incredible, nor a method for ensuring worldly prosperity and success, there is a way forward. We need to be humble enough to hear what God is saying, even when He speaks through failure, sorrow, and pain, and we need to be serious enough to move this quest from the edges to the centre of our thinking.

Think first of the God in whom you believe. Is He really the God of the Bible—the Lord of heaven and earth, who has lived our human life through Jesus Christ, His Son, and is by His Spirit present with us

now ?   Or is He still in some way a local God, bound
to the events of long ago, or to your family home, or
to this nation, or to your present circumstances ?
When you talk of a place, or a person, or a community,
as " God-forsaken," do you really mean it ?   Is God
not there ?   Do you believe that God is merciful and
loving when a plane comes safely in on time, but that
His nature changes when it explodes in mid-air ?
Have you ever a passing thought that though Christ
promises us His acceptance and forgiveness, a vengeful
God may still be lurking for us in the shadows ?

Into these quavering questions comes Jesus Christ
again with His sure word of the Father.   There is
only one God and His nature is " Jesus Christ the same
yesterday, and to-day, and for ever."   He comes to
us along many tracks, but He is limited to none of
them.   When one is closed, or another seems blocked,
He will still find the way to reach us.   If the green
pastures have been for a while closed to us, and the
still waters are a distant mirage, He will find us in
the valley of the shadow, and we " will fear no evil."
It is the same God who is in the middle of the roaring
city and in the quiet country village; the same God who
inspires the mind's adventure into new and dazzling
worlds and lets our infant hearts delight in fantasy.

Think of the wisest, kindest, and most understanding person you know.   Do you believe for a
moment that their character would change, no matter
what you did, or what was done to you ?   And yet we
allow ourselves to think that God—in whom wisdom
and kindness and understanding are absolute and
perfect—somehow changes when we are carried away
into a " strange land."   No ; there the Lord's song
can always be sung, for the Lord is always present

unchanged. " Hast thou not known ? hast thou not heard, that the everlasting God, the Lord, the Creator of the ends of the earth, fainteth not, neither is weary ? there is no searching of his understanding."

The better we train ourselves now to hear *this* voice the more firm will our faith be when we travel to the strange land. If we know the warmth and splendour of the sun, we are not likely to say, when grey days come : " The sun has vanished from the earth " for we know that beyond the clouds it shines unchanged. When John Donne wrestled with his soul to find the assurance of God's everlasting mercy he held this image in mind as he thought about the last journey we have all to take into the strangest land of all :

" I have a sin of fear that when I have spun
My last thread, I shall perish on the shore ;
Swear by thy self that at my death, thy Sun
Shall shine as it shines now, and heretofore ;
And having done that, thou hast done,
   I have no more."

This is our God. And what about our present faith ? Is it the faith the Bible speaks of—central, basic, controlling ? Or is it a side-bet that we make with life, hedging against the possible failure of our ambitions ? Or is it a means to a very secular end—a therapeutic device to bring us greater poise and effectiveness ?

The test is the test of Job. In that dramatic prologue we hear the sneer of Satan : " Doth Job serve God for nought ? " Men will trust in God only for what they can get out of it in the way of prosperity, happiness, and success. This satanic theology is still with us. The answer of the Book of Job is to show us a man flung violently into the " strange land," tempted to " curse God and die," ready to argue with the Almighty, but still, still retaining his basic faith, expressed at its noblest in the climactic words : " Though he slay me, yet will I trust in him."

This is the faith that Christ awakens in our souls. For we cannot bargain with Him, as Jacob did with his God. " *If* God will be with me, and will keep me in this way that I go, and will give me bread to eat, and raiment to put on, so that I come again to my father's house in peace ; *then* shall the Lord be my God." We do not set the conditions. Christ does. " If any man will come after me, let him deny himself, and take up his cross, and follow me." To know the eternal strength of the living God, to be able to sing His song in the " strange land," we must commit ourselves without condition to His Christ, and follow where He leads.

" How shall we sing the Lord's song in a strange land ? " The question sounded across the ancient world from " the waters of Babylon." And five hundred years later it found its answer in a prison-cell in Rome. There lay another exile, another Hebrew captive, upon whose hopes and glowing ambitions a door had slammed shut forever. And there Paul dictated to Epaphroditus, to the Church at Philippi, to the whole Christian world—and to you and me—the Lord's song that no power on earth could smother : " I have learned, in whatsoever state I am, therewith to be content. I know both how to be abased, and I know how to abound : every where and in all things I am instructed both to be full and to be hungry, both to abound and to suffer need. I can do all things through Christ which strengtheneth me."

XII

ALONE BUT NOT LONELY

"I will not leave you comfortless : I will come to you."—
JOHN XIV. 18.

WITH these simple words we are given the secret of the vitality of the Christian faith. When we really hear them, we know why it is that in the mid-twentieth century men and women are finding the same confidence and courage that animated Peter and Paul; the same dynamic of love that was in John, and Francis of Assisi, and Wesley, and David Livingstone; the same intellectual satisfaction as Origen, Augustine, Aquinas and John Calvin experienced. " I will not leave you comfortless : I will come to you." The Founder of our faith is alive. He has not abandoned His followers, and left them with only a memory to inspire them, only a ceremony to encourage them, only a Book to guide them. As surely as He appeared in the flesh as an infant in the Bethlehem stable, He appears now and always in the Spirit to those who believe.

No other religious leader has given a promise like this : " I will come to you." In recent years we have learned much about other Jewish sects that flourished about the time of Christ. We cannot claim that all the teaching of Jesus, and the ideas that gathered around Him and ran like wildfire through the minds of His disciples, are entirely unique. From the Dead Sea Scrolls and other documents we learn of religious communities that spoke a similar language, and bristled with the same explosive ideas. Any Roman student of Semitic religion who happened to bump into the first Christian churches would have classified them at once as just another fringe sect of the Jews. I heard a TV discussion recently in which representatives of different religious views spoke of the new understanding of the origins of Christianity, and their conclusion seemed to be that somehow the uniqueness of Christianity had been exploded. But surely the greatest question to be answered is simply this : How did one among many religious sects in the Middle East nineteen hundred years ago develop into the most universal and world-transforming faith that man has ever known ? The answer does not lie in historical accident, nor in the appeal of its ceremonies, nor even in the power of its teaching. The answer lies solely in the Person of its Founder. What is unique in Christianity is Jesus Christ—and the promise He fulfilled to come and to remain as the living Lord of His Church. We worship, and others are worshipping in Africa, in Asia, in nearly every language that exists, because our Lord is not a memory to be disinterred from ancient scrolls, but a living and abiding presence in His Church and in our hearts. " I will not leave you comfortless : I will come to you." He has come. He is here.

I wonder how many in the Church, or on the edge of the Church, to-day are missing the real meaning of the Gospel just because they have never taken these words seriously, never understood the full force of Christ's claim to be present *now*, to be giving us *now* the whole resources of God's love—everything that He represented during His days on earth ? It is so easy to have the skin and bones of a religion, like a stuffed whale in a glass case in a museum—all whale, but all dead. It is quite common to have a confined religion, sporadically active—like that little captive whale at Coney Island, splashing around in its pool, and kept alive by occasional shots through the epidermis. But the Christian faith, as promised in the Gospels and lived by its saints, is the great live whale of the ocean, pulsing with an inner vitality, plunging in freedom through the vast sustaining waters—exuberant, and tingling with the spirit of life. Nothing less than that is the hope held out before us, a religion that is buoyant with confidence in the Father Almighty, liberated by the touch of Christ the Son, and animated and directed by the Holy Spirit, the Lord and Giver of Life.

Such a religion rests on this simple promise of its Founder : " I will not leave you comfortless : I will come unto you." These words mean much more than an assurance of some kind of spiritual comfort in times of trouble. They are directed to our fundamental condition as human beings, and convey the eternal answer of the Gospel with living, contemporary force.

" I will not leave you *comfortless* "—the word is " orphans," and the Greek implies abandonment, isolation, desolation, utter loneliness. " Comfortless," in our modern speech, has lost these terrible overtones. It merely suggests being deprived of the sympathy and understanding we need. To some it might mean no more than to be left without those external comforts that our society has come to rely on. (I saw in a church notice the other day the words : " Worship in air-conditioned comfort.") What our Lord is speaking about is nothing less than the deepest pit into which we can fall—the last loneliness of the soul cut off from man, cut off from God. The " comfortless " are the derelict, the God-forsaken. To be " comfortless " is to be like Job, crying out in his agony : " O that I knew where I might find him." To be " comfortless " is to descend into the hell where all other prayer is blotted out by the terrible words : " My God, why hast thou forsaken me ? " And that, remember, was a hell that Jesus was to know.

Perhaps it may seem rather extreme to speak of this as our fundamental condition as human beings. We may seldom, or never, have reached the point when we feel totally abandoned by God and man. We may not have been with King Lear out on the wind-swept heath with the " Never, never, never, never, never " ringing in our ears, or have drifted with the Ancient Mariner into the stagnant sea where neither God nor man gave sign of life. Yet everyone of us has been lonely, and the sting of loneliness is just this threat of abandonment, the feeling that there is no one in heaven or earth who cares. Every one of us is launched out into this mysterious world alone, but it was the union of two people that brought us into being, from the beginning we were surrounded with love and care, and in our journey onwards we feed continually on that which is beyond ourselves. However self-reliant and independent we become we crave a presence that is not ourselves, someone somewhere who responds. To be lonely may be only a passing mood, but deep down we know instinctively that to be ultimately lonely is to be lost.

I.A.P.—8

Loneliness is then a spiritual condition. It cannot be remedied simply by producing another person or another million persons. It is therefore quite different from being alone. One New Year's Eve, before I came to live here, I was passing through New York and found myself at midnight on Times Square. In the surrounding streets there were about a million people, and I was right in the middle of them. Yet at that moment I realized as never before that there is perhaps no place where a man or woman can be so utterly lonely as in the midst of a crowd. Imagine someone there, with no background faith, no home in heaven or earth to believe in, no sense of any man or God who cared—lonely, but not alone. The physical presence of a million fellow-beings could only add to the desolation of the soul.

Yet how persistently we try to seek a remedy for loneliness by trying not to be alone. There are perhaps few places on earth where it is more difficult to be alone than New York—and few places where it is easier to be lonely. It looks as though a multitude of lonely people had entered into a conspiracy to banish their loneliness by never being alone. We can wake to the chatter of the radio, herd together on subways and buses, eat in crowded restaurants and drugstores, sit with a thousand others in the dark anonymity of a movie-house, spend the evening at a party, and fall asleep to the sound of a Late-late show. And through it all we can be more lonely than a shepherd on the Outer Hebrides, or a lighthouse-keeper off the coast of Maine. Comfortless—with all the comforts of our modern life.

If it is true that there are more lonely people than ever in our society to-day then the reason is certainly not to be found in our isolation. If the cure lay in not being alone we should all have found it. We are not alone—and yet so many are lonely. Surely it is clear that the trouble—and the remedy—lies within ? And, if that is so, perhaps the first step that the lonely modern has to take is to learn again to be alone.

We can never reach the point where the ultimate threat of loneliness can be removed from us so long as we are running away from ourselves. For that is what so often we are doing in our constant sociability. We run away from ourselves because we are not quite sure who we really are—and whether anybody cares. We are afraid to stop and look—in case there is nobody there. When the Prodigal Son was in the far country with plenty of money he would never be alone. He plunged from party to party, from thrill to thrill, surrounded by the good-time boys and girls—and in the midst of it all he was lost. He was lost, said Jesus, as surely as the coin that rolled away into a crack in the floor, or the sheep that wandered off from the flock on to the mountainside. But when the money ran out he had to stop. " He came to himself," said Jesus. Now at last, in rags, and feeding from the trough with the swine, he was alone. And for the first time he ceased to be lonely. For as he came to himself there came to him a vision of his real home. " And he arose, and came to his father. But when he was yet a great way off, his father saw him, and had compassion, and ran, and fell on his neck, and kissed him."

" I will not leave you comfortless : I will come unto you." We need to be alone to hear that voice, to know the Presence that ends all loneliness. In

prayer, in worship, in a time of crisis, a time of deep
sorrow, a time of holy joy, a time of deep anxiety—
or just at any moment that conscience speaks we need
to turn and meet ourselves. And there, when we
come to ourselves, we can find our God coming to us
—and know that loneliness is swallowed up in an
everlasting love.

When Jesus spoke these words the disciples were
very much alone. They knew that they were listening
to a farewell talk from their Master. They knew that,
after the glory and excitement of the campaign cul-
minating in the triumphal entry into Jerusalem, they
were going to be left as a cluster of leaderless, floundering creatures, with no programme, no policy, no
hopes—orphans of the diabolical storm that was then
raging in Jerusalem. But their Lord had other plans.
" I will not leave you orphans : I will come to you."
They did not fully realize what He meant—no, not
even after they saw Him risen from the dead ; for
again He vanished from their sight. They did not
really know what He meant till that day when the
Spirit of Christ swept into their lives like the wind
of heaven and glowed in their hearts like tongues of
fire. Then they were welded into a company from
which loneliness was banished for ever. Alone, with
the Spirit of Christ, they set out to conquer the world
for Him.

None of us normally desires to be alone—except
for those essential moments when we meet with ourselves and with our God. Our natural instinct is for
companionship. " It is not good that the man should
be alone," says the Lord in the Genesis creation-
story—and so Eve comes into being. Yet none of us

can escape the experience of finding ourselves unexpectedly alone ; and that is the testing time. Being
alone can be like walking in an empty valley with the
clouds of loneliness threatening to enshroud us ; or
it can be like standing on the mountain-peak with
the solid rock beneath us, and the eternal light striking
through the clouds. " I will not leave you comfortless :
I will come to you."

Sometimes we must choose to be alone. There are
occasions when the Christian, for conscience' sake, must
stand alone against the strong tide of surrounding
passion and opinion. Like Martin Luther at the Diet
of Worms, he must be prepared to defy the pressure
of the times and say : " Here stand I : I can do no
other : so help me God." That is no ancient tale.
Exactly the same stand is taken to-day in East
Germany by a boy or girl who refuses to participate
in the Communist Youth Dedication ceremony, and
chooses confirmation in the Christian Church. And
every one of us, if we are loyal, will know some moment
when we must take a lone stand for our beliefs. This
is the " fiery furnace " that the author of the Book of
Daniel describes, the testing time for our convictions.
And you remember what the end of that story was.
Three men, who stood alone for their faith, cast bound
into the fiery furnace . . . then " Lo, I see four men
loose . . . and the form of the fourth is like the Son
of God." " I will not leave you comfortless : I will
come to you." Throughout history to our own day,
it is the testimony of the saints that He has come.

But, much more often, we do not choose to be alone.
Suddenly, unexpectedly, we are left alone. It is then
that we need the grace to turn what looks like a closed
door of desolation into the threshold of a new and

deeper life. For to be thus alone can for a moment
overwhelm us : then it can be the still point where,
as never before, we can hear the voice that banishes
loneliness for ever. " I will not leave you comfortless :
I will come to you."

This is the vitality of the Christian faith. From the
eternal companionship of the living God—Father, Son,
and Holy Spirit—there comes the assurance that
there is no loneliness in the Kingdom of His love.
Christ walked that way once for us alone so that none
of us need ever be left desolate. And He is not just
another holy memory of a good man long ago. He is
alive to meet us now in the fulfilment of His promise :
" I will not leave you comfortless : I will come to
you."

XIII

THE CALM IN OUR CONFUSION

A PALM SUNDAY ADDRESS

" And when he was come near, he beheld the city, and wept over it, Saying, If thou hadst known, even thou, at least in this thy day, the things which belong unto thy peace ! but now they are hid from thine eyes."—LUKE XIX. 41. 42.

" THE things which belong unto thy peace "—what are these things ?

The nations of the world want to know—as never before, for they know what the penalty of not finding them can be. In every country responsible citizens are asking : What is the way ? Strength to maintain the nuclear stalemate ? Controlled disarmament ? Total disarmament ? An international police-force ? In a totally new situation for diplomacy, an unprecedented alignment and distribution of power, what are the things which belong to our peace ?

And within each nation we want to know. The pictures flash across our screen. Ugly incidents at drugstore counters, probes into dishonesty and deceit, murder-trials, divorces, elopements, riots in South Africa, a barbed-wire frontier of hatred running right through the middle of the city over which Jesus wept— all these, and the pictures we never see of the muzzled or imprisoned victims of dictatorship, are enough to

make any sensitive man or woman yearn after the
things which belong to our peace.

Most of all within ourselves we want to know.   For
these disturbing events of the outside world are often
not much more to us than a kind of distant reverbera-
tion of a discord in our own breasts.   We are so made
that an explosion of violence and bloodshed three
thousand miles away, or even a murder in the next
block, will affect us less than a minor disagreement with
someone in our home or office ; and racial and international tensions seem as nothing to the tensions that
build up in our own souls.   When we are distracted by
our personal problems, these world events flicker behind
us like the pictures on drive-in movie screens that we
rush past in the night.   Even if we have no major personal worry gnawing at our hearts we are liable to be
confused and bewildered by the mere rush of everyday
events.   How do we sort out the relative importance
of the things we are doing ?   How do we discover
our own true selves in the whirlpool of our social
contacts ?   How do we find the still centre to give
meaning to all our restless activities ?   Or must we fill
in the first blank in our census-papers by writing :
" My name is Legion ; for we are many " ?   In the
clatter and distraction of our daily life in this city
what are the things that belong to our peace ?   Tran-
quillizers ?   Alcohol ?   Self-help booklets ?   Or what ?

Anyone who offers a quick solution to the questions
of world peace, racial tensions, social disorders, or
disturbed minds and consciences is a quack.   Solutions
to major problems in society have always been worked
out with blood and sweat and tears, and if we find
some short-cut to give us complete personal happiness
and serenity in the midst of the agony of others we

have reached a phoney peace. When the cry of the world's suffering reaches me I don't want to be offered an ear-plug; when the threat of disaster looms up black I don't want rose-tinted glasses. And if my own disquiet is caused by some wrong I am doing to others, I don't want to compound that wrong by drugging my conscience into a blissful detachment.

There is a dimension here—in suffering and in evil —that cannot be penetrated by any surface therapy, or reached by any lightning cure. The prophet Jeremiah had something to say about this phoney peace : " For they have healed the hurt of the daughter of my people slightly, saying, Peace, peace ; when there is no peace."

At the same time with all my being I revolt against the man who tells me that peace is a pious dream, and that the things which belong to it are sheer illusion. There is a danger that those who reject the slick solutions of a phoney peace may be tempted to deny all possibility of reaching an inner calm or of healing the conflicts that divide mankind. We are threatened with the bleak and cynical formulae of a so-called objectivism that teaches us to scorn the ideals by which men have lived and to revert to the philosophy of the jungle. Nature, " red in tooth and claw ", is objective enough, but the whole story of man is of his struggle to impose on it an order, a meaning, and a peace that comes from an equally objective but a higher source. The men and women who have earned the respect and admiration of us all have been those who have had about them some aura of an inward peace and have been able to bring into the jungle a quieting and a reconciling power. There *is* a peace to be discovered, a calm in our confusion, and a reservoir of hope and healing for the world. It is the peace of God—a peace which, so far from being a push-button solution to all our troubles, is truly described as the peace " which passeth all understanding."

" If thou hadst known," said Jesus, as He looked across the valley to the great marble Temple, sparkling in the spring sunshine, and to the cluster of rooftops that covered the seething life of the city He loved, " If thou hadst known, even thou, in this thy day, the things which belong unto thy peace." This was the peace He was speaking of—the " peace of God, which passeth all understanding," the peace that is reached *in* confusion, the peace that is found *through* pain, the peace that is stronger than the forces of malice, hatred, and revenge.

" If thou hadst known . . ." The tragedy of mankind is in these words. The things that belong to our peace were there that day—in the person of Jesus Christ. He had taught them and He had lived them. In Him the Kingdom of God had come to earth, and its message of peace is radically simple—doing the will of God. " Thy kingdom come. Thy will be done on earth, as it is in heaven." Jesus just did the Father's will. And He invited all to seek it and to do it too. There was peace in it, and joy, and spiritual power, but He never asked us to make these our chief aim in life. " Seek ye first the kingdom of God," He said, " and all these things shall be added unto you."

That was what brought Him to Jerusalem on this first Palm Sunday, to a city where His enemies had already plotted His arrest, where the Roman stood ready with a cross, and where the crowd was fickle as an April sky. As He stood there facing the city there was a peace shimmering behind Him, the mirage of Galilee that must have reached the inward eye. How easy to turn back, to withdraw from the maelstrom of plots and politics, passion and confusion that was Jerusalem. But there was another peace in front of Him—a peace that passed all understanding. And the path to it lay through that threatening city, and out again to the Garden of Gethsemane and the hill called Calvary. For Him this was the way of His Father's will. His human instincts clamoured for another way—" O my Father, if it be possible, let this cup pass from me : nevertheless not as I will, but as thou wilt. "With this heroic acceptance came that deep mysterious peace which has been His legacy to all who follow.

Here is one thing that belongs to our peace—a Christ-like courage. How different this is from our usual image of Christian peace of mind :

> " O Sabbath rest by Galilee !
> O calm of hills above."

There was no rest for Jesus as He rode into the seething city of Jerusalem, and there was no calm on that Mount of Olives where the very stones cried out. The calm was only to be found in a mind set like a flint to do the Father's will, and a conscience clear as the noonday sun. This peace is not an escape-hatch through which we slip away : it is the by-product of a decision to do, here at the danger-point, what we know within us to be right. As Studdert Kennedy put it :

> " Peace does not mean the end of all our striving,
> Joy does not mean the drying of our tears ;
> Peace is the power that comes to souls arriving
> Up to the light where God Himself appears."

Some little time ago I read in the *New York Times* that a friend of mine, Joost de Blank, who is now Archbishop in South Africa, had refused to let the Anglican Church there join in a national day of prayer in the present crisis. " It must be categorically stated," he said, " that a Day of Prayer must never be called as an escape into inactivity. . . . The Church of the Province of South Africa therefore regards as hypocritical a corporate Day of Prayer so long as certain sponsoring churches have not openly denounced the primary evil causes of the present distress." If Joost de Blank had wanted a peaceful life he would never have made such a statement. But we—whatever our knowledge or ignorance of the South African situation—can recognize the courage of a man who follows the dictates of his Christian conscience and must know that deeper peace that passes all normal understanding.

Pastor Niemoeller could have had peace with the Nazis ; Bishop Dibelius, in Berlin, could to-day have peace with the East German Communist régime. For both men nothing much was required—just a little adjustment of their Christian convictions. But each chose to follow the way of conscience and conviction and chose, not the peace of quiet compromise, but the Peace of the Passion.

You and I may never be faced with such public and resounding choices, yet every one of us knows the temptation of the little compromise, the minor adjustment of conscience for the sake of what we call " peace." And everyone, I hope, has also known at times something of that other peace that comes after a hard decision has been taken and we have done what we know to be right. A Christ-like courage is one of " the things which belong to our peace."

But there is something else. This peace is reached not only through courage and honesty in our dealings with our fellow-men : it comes with an attitude of childlike trust in our Father-God. In the person of Christ Himself—and in His communicated and in-fectious grace—these two are inseparably joined. The gift of courage in our daily decisions flows from an inward faith in God : and such an inward faith is not truly Christian unless it provides such strength. We have before us the image of courage among men— Christ with His eyes fixed upon the city of danger and death, and set to travel the Via Dolorosa in the sole light of His Father's will. Let me give you another image that may serve as a symbol of the inner peace and trust that possessed Him then.

A few days ago I found myself rushing from a Presbytery meeting to keep another appointment. As I dived down the subway I just missed a North-bound express and began to pace the platform. It could have been a moment for quiet reflection—but the 14th Street Subway Station is not exactly the Taj Mahal, and I was soon part of a growing crowd of tense, impatient, restless citizens in a wilderness of chewing-gum machines. Trains clattered by on other lines, brakes squealed, harsh voices argued, and anxious heads peered into the dark tunnel as if to extract the coaches for which we were all feverishly waiting. Sud-denly I felt that someone was looking at me. I turned and met the wide-open, unblinking blue eyes of a six-month-old infant, lying peacefully in his mother's arms. He was completely undisturbed by the noise, and in those blue eyes there was not the slightest reflection of the nervous anxious glances all around him. It was as if he said to me : " What are you all worried about ? Where I came from a couple of minutes here and there means nothing at all. Look ; I'm in my mother's arms and I trust her completely. Have you nothing to rest on, no one to trust ? "

" Verily I say unto you, Whosoever shall not receive the kingdom of God as a little child shall in no wise enter therein."

A Christ-like courage—yes, and a childlike trust are among " the things " which belong to our peace. When we have really faced the implications of true discipleship we are ready to hear again about this simple trust. If some smug, contented, comfortable person, who has known little sorrow, were to tell us in our troubles to trust in God, we could brush it off as sentimental twaddle. But it is the warrior saints who bring us this word. It is men and women who have been on the edge of despair, victims of pain, of cruelty and injustice. And supremely it is Jesus Christ who wept over the city that was about to destroy Him, who saw the flames of cruelty lurking in the eyes of the crowd, and of desertion in the eyes of His friends. It was He who said : " Why are ye so fearful ? Have faith in God."

How can mature, sophisticated men and women get back to a child-like trust, like that infant who lay quietly as the calm in our confusion ? How do we reach to what T. S. Eliot has called " the still point in the turning world " ? " How can a man be born when he is old ? " asked Nicodemus, " Can he enter the second time into his mother's womb, and be born ? '

" Marvel not that I said unto thee, Ye must be born again," said Jesus, " The wind bloweth where it listeth, and thou hearest the sound thereof, but canst not tell whence it cometh, and whither it goeth : so is every one that is born of the Spirit."

There is a new birth possible for us all. The living Spirit of God, invisible and powerful as the wind, is present now, and at all times, to re-create and re-direct our lives. That is why we pray : that is why we worship. As we empty ourselves of all else, letting go the earthly supports to which we cling, and the claim to run our lives by ourselves alone ; and as we turn to the living Christ through whom God speaks to us to-day, we shall begin to know this thing that belongs to our peace—that God is the Father in whom we can have an absolute trust.

" If thou hadst known . . ." By God's grace we have been given the chance to know, to know the things that belong to our peace, and to the peace of our world—a child-like trust in the Father in heaven, and a Christ-like courage to meet the challenges of our day, and the decisions of our daily life. If we will rest our final hopes, even in the darkness, in the God and Father of Jesus Christ, and if we are prepared to do what is shown to us to be right in spite of the dangers ahead, then we shall know the peace that passes all understanding. For this is the message of Palm Sunday and Passion Week. This is the legacy of Christ. " Peace I leave with you, my peace I give unto you : not as the world giveth, give I unto you. Let not your heart be troubled, neither let it be afraid."

XIV

MACHINES, MAGIC, AND MYSTERY

A LENTEN ADDRESS

" And God said unto Moses, I AM THAT I AM."—EXODUS III. 14.

THE season of Lent might be defined by an outside observer as the period when some Christians try to take their religion seriously. One of the reasons why our Presbyterian forefathers refused to observe most of these seasons and festivals was that they believed that religion is utterly central and serious every moment of our life ; that for the Christian all of life is Lent, every day is Good Friday, every hour is Easter, every moment a potential Pentecost.

While most of us would agree that the Protestant churches have been right to restore the rhythm of the major seasons and holy days to our life and worship, we have to confess that, in part, we need them because we have lost the all-embracing sense of God's holy presence, and the steady day-by-day conviction that the birth and life, the death and resurrection of Jesus Christ are the central facts on which our lives depend.

So we may welcome Lent if it really does stimulate us to ask again what our religion means to us. By way of preparation, we are going to think now about

what religion means as a basic attitude to life. I
am sure we all know very well, in our heart of hearts,
that dealing with God is either the most important
thing we do, underlying every other activity of our
lives, or else it is an utter illusion, a hang-over from
the childhood of the race. The reason why we fumble
and hesitate, why we allow religion to be just one
interest among others, a part-time or spare-time
activity, is that while we cannot eradicate the religious
instinct from our hearts and minds, we are not wholly,
powerfully, and permanently convinced that God is
real, that this world is penetrated by His presence,
and that our lives and all human history are under His
control. If we were, would we let ourselves be so
elated or depressed by passing events ? If we were,
would we rate our bank-balance above what Jesus
called : " treasure in heaven " ? If we were, would
we ever slacken in our worship or our prayers ?

Here we are, mysteriously alive in a mysterious
universe. Religion has to do with this mystery.
And the more we open ourselves to it, the more deeply
we allow ourselves to be penetrated by it, the surer
we shall become of the reality of God and of the
eternal world. Our real difficulty is not that of fitting
religious convictions into an otherwise tidy picture of
the universe : it is that we habitually live with the
small fragment of the whole that we can see and
touch and measure and do not expose ourselves to the
full impact of the mystery. Religion does not create
the mystery. It is there—at all the crucial points of
our existence, from our first arrival out of the unknown
to the point of departure that is the final question-
mark of life. Why am I here ? Where am I going ?
What is the good life ? Why do we suffer ? What

are these longings for knowledge and for beauty ?
If you tell me these are foolish questions that cannot
be answered I reply that a fly on the wall, or a cow in
the field, may not ask them, but I can and, like my
kinsmen through the ages, I will. For these are the
questions that created the social order, built the
Pyramids and Chartres Cathedral, wrote the plays of
Shakespeare, painted the Mona Lisa, sent men to the
peak of Everest or the depths of the ocean, and have
covered the earth with a rich garment of prayer and
of praise. We begin to live when we are confronted
like Moses with the burning bush, the blazing mystery
at the heart of things which can never be reduced
to the ashes of our material world. And we begin to
know what religion is all about when we hear from
the burning bush the Voice that says : " I AM THAT
I AM."

The trouble with our generation is that we have become too narrow-minded. The last two hundred years
have seen such an amazing advance in knowledge and
technical achievement, an advance that now seems
to be accelerating at a bewildering rate, that we have
tended to interpret ultimate truth in these terms. In
other words, being amazingly successful with machines,
we tend to think that this is also how the universe is
made. Having found one profitable road of explana-
tion and understanding we forget the many others
that have been travelled by the human soul. Until
quite recently it was popularly supposed that human
progress could be measured solely in terms of machines
that could fly faster, produce in greater quantity, or
make a bigger bang. The production of the machine
(quite literally) to end all machines has made us revise

this notion, and to remember that there are other faculties of the human spirit by which progress can be measured.

But not all. We read a short time ago that Mr. Khrushchev, confronted with the exquisite creations of Indonesian art, said : " I don't like anything . . . They represent a bygone day, an era that is past . . . If we go on like this there will be no progress . . . Machines, machines are what you need." I seem to hear what sounds like the final chorus of a new materialist musical. " Machines, machines are all you need." And in the chorus line I recognize not just Marxists, but familiar figures from our own environment :

" Machines, machines, machines are all you need,
  Machines to plough the furrows, machines to sow the
      seed,
  Machines to keep you healthy, machines to entertain,
  Machines to count opinion, machines to wash your
      brain,
  Machines to filter tars in,
  Machines to go to Mars in,
  Machines, machines, machines are all you need,
  Machines to run a church with, machines to say the
      creed."

We mustn't give the impression that our modern machines in themselves are a road-block for religion. The machines, like all other human inventions, are a gift of God to be used with gratitude. But what Mr. Khrushchev expressed is the crude belief that mechaniz-ation is the key to human life—" machines are all you need "—with the implication that the universe itself is one vast impersonal machine. It is the silent infil-tration of *this* belief into our society, into our minds,

that can truly be called subversive, and this is a danger
that cannot be met by reckless and scurrilous charges
such as those recently given publicity concerning
our Protestant churches, but by a vigorous
affirmation of the truths for which these churches
stand.

This universe is not a machine humming and spin-
ning in the darkness, and our part in it is not just to
tinker for a moment with the fraction of it that is
briefly lit up for our convenience. The universe is a
mystery whose radiance can reach the human spirit
and kindle in us a flame of meaning and of hope.
" A man's life," said Jesus, " consisteth not in the
abundance of the *things* that he possesseth " (Luke
XII. 15). For Him what mattered was not the economy
of abundance, but the philosophy of abundance—
the entrance here and now into the Kingdom of God.
" I am come that they might have life, and that they
might have it more abundantly " (John x. 10). He
rejected the narrow world of the materialist with its
anxieties and fears, and responded to the great mystery
of the Kingdom that speaks in the simplest things and
wakes our wonder and our praise. " Consider the lilies
how they grow : they toil not, they spin not ; and yet
I say unto you, that Solomon in all his glory was not
arrayed like one of these " (Luke XII. 27). " Consider
the lilies." You can, if you like, consider them as
a machine ; strip down the petals, and analyse the
stem. The information you obtain is not to be despised.
Someone in our civilization is always called to strip
and analyse the lily : otherwise the discoveries we all
enjoy could not be made. But can we really believe
that *this* is the only true way to consider the lily ?
For Jesus, and for millions since, it is not a machine

but a burning bush, burning with the mystery of God.

We are probably all convinced that we are nearer the truth when we hear religion speak of the mystery than when we are absorbed in the clatter of our machine-age, and the know-how of technology. We would rather stand watching the Niagara Falls with a poet who heard in its thunder the voice of the prophet and saw in its leaping rainbows angel-vestments, than with the mythical Texan who is reported to have said he knew a plumber who could fix it. But, for all this, we are still hesitant about the mystery. We are afraid of magic.

I have sometimes felt, when trying to talk about the Christian faith to an agnostic, that the gleam in his eye if not his actual words implied : " Poor fellow, you are still living in the days of magic. You think there is a Man Upstairs who can do things for you, if you know the right strings to pull. Don't you know that all our progress has been an emancipation from magic and superstition ? We are learning what makes the world tick, and there is no more room for your Man Upstairs."

Fortunately there is an increasing number who can now distinguish between magic and mystery. Of course, our ancestors believed in magic, and there are remnants of magic in all quarters to-day. Magic is an attempt to influence and control the powers of the universe by tricks and devices—incantations, crystal-balls, horoscopes, charms, and secret formulae. As an attempt to find out how the universe works and use it for our ends it is the ancestor of science as well as religion, and an ancestor that clings to our backs like the Old Man of the Sea. But the magic-attitude to the universe is totally different from the mystery-attitude. The essence of belief in magic is an attempt to control some totally irrational power. The essence of belief in mystery is the humble effort to learn through all the senses what lies behind this pattern of things, and to enter into communion with a Divine Spirit that reflects in utter perfection the goodness and wisdom and beauty that is the highest that we know in man. The motivation of the magic-attitude is fear, distrust, and a desire to get : the motivation of the mystery-attitude is wonder, trust, and a desire to be.

The Bible speaks of mystery. This is the way to understand it. Some go to it with the mind of magic. They want to revel in miracles, just as the contemporaries of Jesus did. They did not understand that His miracles were not conjuring-tricks, but signs—signs of the mystery of the Kingdom. Such people want from the Bible magic verses that will help them to material success, or secret information about coming events. Others, again, approach the Bible with the mind of the machine. They dissect it as an ancient piece of literature ; spin theories to account for all its teachings as by-products of something else ; and trim down its mighty pages to the size of their mechanistic minds.

" And God said unto Moses, I AM THAT I AM." This is no magic formula. Nor can we hear what it says if we are too busy tracing the origins of the Hebrew Tetragrammaton. We have to find our burning bush, right where we are, and listen to this voice from the heart of the mystery. For the Bible tells us that the mystery is God. "I AM THAT I AM." Just that.

There is no other definition, for God cannot be described to mortal man. Yet note how the mystery is already more than mystery. It is mystery disclosed. God speaks. How does He speak? In a thousand different ways. But the Bible, in all its amazing variety, is utterly consistent about this : the mystery is disclosed by God. We don't battle our way into His presence. We cannot " by searching find out God." He speaks. And the waiting, trusting, humble spirit hears. " I AM THAT I AM." This is more than mystery. It is the voice from beyond the mystery, a voice that we recognize, for it is the love-call of the Father-God.

The Church of Christ is not set here for mental gymnastics among congenial people. It is the community of God that exists to hear His voice and respond. It would not exist here to-day if God had not called Abraham and said " Get thee out," if He had not said to Moses " I AM THAT I AM," if He had not in the fullness of the time " sent forth his Son "—the fullest disclosure of the mystery that can be made to man. You remember Paul's words to the Ephesians, " Unto me, who am less than the least of all saints, is this grace given, that I should preach among the Gentiles the unsearchable riches of Christ." How did he continue ? " And to make all men see what is the *fellowship of the mystery*, which from the beginning of the world hath been hid in God." This is what we are—" the fellowship of the mystery "—men and women who are called together because we want to know, and to adore, and to respond in love to the mystery that has been illuminated in the life, the death, and the resurrection of Jesus Christ our Lord.

Our church is not a machine for the production of religion. It is not a place where magic spells are cast.

But, by the grace of God, it can become the burning bush in the midst of our concrete wilderness where we may hear the voice that says not only " I AM THAT I AM " but " I am the light of the world : he that followeth me shall not walk in darkness, but shall have the light of life."

XV

THE INEVITABLE CROSS

A Passion Sunday Address

"Now is my soul troubled ; and what shall I say ? Father, save me from this hour : but for this cause came I unto this hour."— JOHN XII. 27.

A FEW years ago *Time-Magazine* printed the results of an enquiry directed to thirty prominent people in America. They were given a hundred famous events in history and asked to list them in order of importance and significance for mankind. The result of the poll was interesting. Top place was given to Columbus' discovery of America. In the fourteenth place three events were placed equal : the discovery of X-rays ; the Wright brothers' first plane flight, and the Crucifixion of Jesus Christ.

Among those making this judgment there must have been various members and adherents of the Christian Church—that is to say, men and women who have countless times confessed in worship their belief that the crucified and risen Christ is the Saviour of the world ; heard the declaration of pardon in the name of Jesus Christ who died for our sins ; received the Holy Communion of the body and blood of the Lord ; and joined in singing such hymns as " In the cross of Christ

I glory, towering o'er the wrecks of time." How do
they reconcile the tremendous affirmations that they
make in church with the sober judgment, made when
their religious guard is down, that the Cross of Christ
shares fourteenth place in order of importance for
mankind ?

I don't know. Every one of us has a share in this
paradox. We all know the difficulty of affirming
boldly in the cold light of the secular world the beliefs
that we sincerely hold—or at least *want* to hold—
when we are in the atmosphere of worship. I spoke
of their " religious guard " being down. You know
how it is. We tend to shelter our religious beliefs
within the walls of the church or of our private devotions. Beyond these we breathe a secular air and
pass secular judgments. If any professing Christian
who took part in that questionnaire had been chal-
lenged about the rating, he might well have answered :
" Of course, this was just a secular judgment. I
wasn't thinking of religion."

What possible right have we to make such a distinction ? A statement concerning the significance
of Jesus Christ cannot be true in Madison Avenue Presbyterian Church, and untrue in Columbia University,
or in Lenox Hill Hospital, or in Wall Street. A
religious truth must be true in the world outside or it
is not a truth at all. And of all the proclamations of
religion there is none so firmly planted in the soil of
secular history as this we make about the Cross of
Christ. This event didn't happen in a church or
temple. It took place in the full light of day " outside
a city wall." It didn't happen in a sacred book, but
" under Pontius Pilate "—and solidly fixed in human
history as any event of which we say " in the reign of

Henry VIII " or " when Khrushchev was master in the Kremlin."

We have to ask, then, what we really mean when we speak of the Cross. Is it a unique event which changed the course of history, and can change the course of your life and mine to-day ? Or is it an ancient symbol to which we pay respect in church, but which has little place in our everyday thinking ? Was Paul right when he came into ancient Corinth declaring : " I am determined not to know anything among you, save Jesus Christ and him crucified " ? Or was Bernard Shaw right when he dismissed what he called " Crosstianity " as a product of the diseased imagination of this same Paul ?

Many of my sermons, particularly at the Lenten season, end with some kind of reference to the Cross. This is not because I feel the necessity to make a final bow to orthodox doctrine no matter how far our thoughts may have ranged. It is because every preacher who derives his essential message from the Scriptures is magnetically drawn to this central mystery of which they speak—the death of the Son of God. And it is also because, the more experience one has of life, the more we find the true answers to lie in the profundities that cannot be expressed in the surface logic of the mind. We discover that the Bible is entirely right when it says that the preaching of the Cross, which can be offensive to the moralist, and ridiculous to the sophisticated, becomes to the believer both the power and the wisdom of God.

And so on Passion Sunday we begin with the Cross, and we stay with the Cross. For the preacher it is inevitable, inescapable : and not only for the preacher.

Anyone who is drawn with an open mind towards the
way of Christ will find it impossible to avoid a reckoning
with the fact that His life was cut short about the age
of thirty by an ignominious Roman execution. For
the Jewish people to whom He belonged such a death
was not only a physical but a spiritual horror—and
inconceivable for One who claimed to be God's Messiah.
For the philosophers and religious teachers of the
Graeco-Roman world it was an absurdity to suppose
that God could reveal Himself in such a sordid event.
Yet the New Testament writers—in Gospels and
Epistles—not only make no attempt to hush the
matter up ; they go out of their way to describe the
Crucifixion in vivid detail and return to it again and
again as the compulsive centre of their new-found
faith.

So it has been in the witness of the Church from the
beginning. In the first Christian sermon on the day of
Pentecost, Peter rose up before the crowd and said
quite bluntly : " You killed Him—but God has raised
Him up." From Jerusalem the story has fanned out
over the entire world and has spoken to the conscience
of all mankind. And always there has been this note
of our personal implication in this deed : " You killed
Him—but look what God has done and can do for
you." No one can claim to be seriously concerned
with Christianity and escape this inevitable Cross.
In every age attempts are made to bury it in some
cave like the Dead Sea Scrolls, and to construct a
faith based simply on the teaching of Jesus. But as
Paul said to King Herod Agrippa : " This thing
was not done in a corner "—and the Cross rears up
again against the Calvary sky, inevitable, inescapable,
and demanding a decision.

Authentic Christianity—as we see from the hymns, creeds, and prayers of the universal Church and the lives of all its saints—has always known that the Cross speaks to us the unique word of Jesus Christ. It is the climax of His teaching. It is inseparable from His life. It is the point to which the whole Bible story leads and from which the Christian Church starts out. No matter how attractive some diluted versions of the faith may be with their elimination of the Cross and their appeal to our desire for a simple ethical code by which to live, they lack the dimension that only this word can bring. For the preaching of the Cross has overtones that can be heard in those depths which no simple ethics or logic can reach.

On a bright April afternoon fifteen years ago I conducted a funeral service for two prisoners-of-war who had died of starvation and exhaustion. A thin procession, headed by an old farm-cart, passed out through the gates of a camp that lay under a pall of gloom and despair—the darkest hour before the dawn of liberation. We headed slowly for a little wood a mile away. Half-way there the little cortège broke into a trot to avoid a sudden swooping attack by six of our own planes. I spoke the words of committal to the sound of strafing just beyond the wood, and the bodies were lowered into a rough hole in the ground. Five years prisoners, living on hope, and now they lay in this deserted wood. No human words can say anything—only the words that come from the One with nail-prints in His hands : " I am the resurrection and the life."

Two summers ago I stood on that same spot. The old camp is now a flourishing little town of refugees from East Germany. And when I took the road again and traced the path to the little wood I found a most beautiful and well-tended cemetery. There the men I had buried lay with other prisoners from America, from Britain, from France, and from Russia and with them were the new graves of German refugees. And above them all rising on a simple arch at the entrance-gate rose a large plain cross. In the sunshine of that day there fell upon the graves of so-called friend and foe, upon the memories of a common suffering and a mysterious fate, the shadow of Calvary. There is no other place to understand such things.

" Now is my soul troubled ; and what shall I say ? Father, save me from this hour : but for this cause came I unto this hour." When we begin to understand the power of this inevitable Cross to speak where men's cleverest words are " as sounding brass or a tinkling cymbal," we find new meaning in the mysterious force that seemed to impel our Lord along that Via Dolorosa. Now that it has happened, the Cross is unavoidable for us. Its mark is set deep in human history, and our common life bears the scar of this Divine sacrifice, this judgment, and this tremendous sympathy. But the question rises : Was it inevitable for Him ? Could Jesus have escaped His Cross ?

No one can read the last chapters of our Four Gospels without a sense that events are moving with an inexorable precision to the determined end. From the moment that Peter confesses Him as Christ, and He sets His face to go to Jerusalem, the words of Jesus are of His appointed end, and everything that happens thereafter seems to contribute with a terrible inevitability to His fate. " The Son of man goeth as it is written of him."

What kind of inevitability is this ? *Is it the inevitability of what we call Fate*—with a capital " F " ?
Did Jesus go to His Cross because He and Pilate and
Judas (and you and I) are all helpless victims of a
prearranged plan—actors in a film that has already
been shot, flickering across the screen to play our
appointed parts ?

" The Moving Finger writes ; and having writ
Moves on : nor all thy Piety nor Wit
Shall lure it back to cancel half a Line,
Nor all thy Tears wash out a Word of it."

The philosophy of Omar Khayyam is totally foreign
to the Gospels. Read the story again and you will find
that none of the men involved are considered the mere
victims of our inscrutable Fate. Whatever mysterious
words the Bible uses about the controlling pattern of
our lives, it always shows us men and women as responsible agents, capable of choice ; and our environment is not the steely chamber of our implacable
Fate, but the presence of the living God. Judas
might have refused the bribe ; the Sanhedrin might
have decided not to condemn ; Pilate may well have
tossed a mental coin before he said : " Set Barabbas
free." And Jesus ? Was there no real conflict in His
spirit, no other avenue really open to Him ? " Now is
my soul troubled ; and what shall I say ? Father, save
me from this hour ? " Was that prayer a mockery ?
—as all prayer must be if Fate is in control ?

It seems to me quite plain that when He had spoken
these words, He could have summoned up supernatural power to dominate the situation, as once
before in His home-town, when the mob was ready to
lynch Him we read that " he passing through the midst

of them went his way " (Luke IV. 30). Isn't this what
He meant when He said in Gethsemane : " Do you
think that I cannot appeal to my Father, and he will
at once send me more than twelve legions of angels ? "
(Matt. XXVI. 53 [R.S.V.]). And it seems equally plain
that instead of going to Gethsemane that night He could
have continued on over the Mount of Olives and taken
the Galilee road which must have lain open and
inviting in the light of the Passover moon.

No : there was no inevitability dictated by Fate.
Was it then what we call *the inevitability of circumstance and human folly* ? There are times in history
when a tragedy happens which need not have happened—except for the apparently inevitable combination of circumstance and men's mistakes. Winston
Churchill has called World War II the " unnecessary
war." It need not have happened. It was not decreed
by Fate. And yet the follies of the 'thirties—the
blindness of the peaceful, the skill and power of the
wicked, and the indifference of masses—produced
together the circumstances that sparked the con-
flagration. Did Jesus die, then, as a result of the
crimes and follies of men and nations, adding up to a
situation where He was their inevitable victim ?

It looks rather like it. How many on Palm Sunday
in Jerusalem—if a poll had been taken—really wanted
Him to be crucified ? Probably not more than a hand-
ful. Yet a week later it had happened. The Pharisees
would probably not have wanted such a violent course,
but they were trapped in the net of their prestige.
The Sadducees were not blood-thirsty scoundrels but
they had a strong political motivation to eliminate
trouble with the Roman power. Pilate had no animus
against Jesus whatever—but his job came first, and

the reports that might be sent to Rome. These
accidents combined with a sudden weakness and
treachery within the group of His disciples to make
the Crucifixion a foregone conclusion. So this is how
it happened ? With this kind of inevitability ?

If this were the true answer we should expect the
Crucifixion to be described as a terrible accident, and
Jesus portrayed as a hapless victim. But there is not
a line of this kind in the record. Jesus moves through
the network of crime and circumstance with the sure
step of one who knows what He is doing and what will
be done to Him. The agony of decision is not the less
real. " Now is my soul troubled ; and what shall I
say ? " This is not an inhuman demi-god for whom
pain, and loneliness, and the brutal curtain of death
mean nothing. He shares with us the shrinking and the
agony. Yet through the tumult of His soul, and the
dark temptations that flooded back with the demons
of the wilderness inviting Him to take another way,
there sounded the calm strong voice of ultimate decision. " Now is my soul troubled ; and what shall I
say ? Father, save me from this hour : but for this
cause came I unto this hour."

" For this cause." With these words His destiny is
clear. He came to die. The Cross which was now
almost within sight would be freely chosen. Why ?
Because there was no other way in which He could
reach to the depth of the human agony He came to
share, could " bear our griefs and carry our sorrows."
And because there was no other way in which He could
draw upon Himself the hopeless weight of our sins,
and expose and absorb the evil that blocks us from the
holiness of God. " The Lord hath laid on him the
iniquity of us all." The only way a God of perfect

I.A.P.—10

peace and joy can reach His suffering family is in this amazing way to share that suffering. The only way a God of perfect purity and goodness can reach His disobedient people is to offer Himself the sacrifice for sin. What we see in the Cross is not the hideous outworking of blind fatality, nor a tragic accident of history. We see the end-result of God's redeeming love going out to seek us where we are. " For this cause came I into the world." *The inevitability is the inevitability of love.*

This is why the story of the Cross, for those who have ears to hear, is the greatest story in the world, and why whenever we hear it we face a life-or-death decision. For the Christ who died brings us right up against the ultimate choice. Faced with this demonstration of God's love, do I continue to grasp my life for myself and to go on to die? Or do I yield myself to Him who loved me and gave Himself for me, and so go on to live ? " Now is *my* soul troubled and what whall I say ? Father, save me from this hour—let me forget about this Cross, let me go my own way ? " " But for this cause came I unto this hour." We know that we have been brought again to face this Cross because by surrendering to this God we find the secret of an unselfish and eternal life. " If any man will come after me," said Jesus, " let him deny *himself*, and take up his cross daily, and follow me. For whosoever will save his life shall lose it : but whosoever will lose his life for my sake, the same shall save it."

XVI

INVULNERABILITY

"And who is he that will harm you, if ye be followers of that which is good?"—I PETER III. 13.

THERE is a dream that haunts the human race—invulnerability. To be invulnerable, unwoundable, unable to be hurt or harmed, to find some magic cloak that will protect us from all danger; this is what we long for. We dream about it, we spin our myths, we play our games, and in a thousand ways we try to make the dream come true. Invulnerability—the point where we are secure, utterly secure.

Watch the little boy as he pulls an old curtain round his shoulder, brandishes his wooden sword, and plunges into the fray. "You can't touch me! You can't touch me! It's a magic cloak." Listen to the stories he reads—the knights whose armour is proof against the most venomous fiery dragon, the hero whose "strength was as the strength of ten, because his heart was pure," the princess who is so beautiful no evil can touch her. The world of fairy-tales is not by any means always a pleasant world. It is filled with witches and dragons and nasty characters of every description. But there's also the protection, the magic cloak, the shield of invulnerability.

We grow up. We graduate from fairy-tales to the myths of Greece and Rome, and then to real history. And we learn some facts of life. The magic cloak is wrapped away with the toys and we learn instead about Achilles' heel. Still the dream of invulnerability—but with a difference. When Achilles' mother dipped him in the River Styx as a baby he became invulnerable—except for the heel by which she held him. And, of course, it was through that tendon he received the fatal wound. Invulnerable? Not quite—and that " not quite " is enough to shake our confidence. This is our world. There is no wrapping of complete security. No magic cloak can stretch down to cover that vulnerable heel. There is always some point where we are open to attack, some crack through which the wound can come.

We know; but we don't want to know it. We cling to the magic cloak, always hoping that there is some way of insuring ourselves from outside. The more dangerous and aggressive the world around us seems to be the more we long for the absolute defence, the invulnerable protection. Instead of recognizing that we are all born with the Achilles' heel of our mortal state and going out gaily to meet the slings and arrows, we tend to grope around for the covering of absolute security.

In the Spring of 1940 the Highland Division with which I was serving was attached to the French Army and we took up position on the Moselle. I well remember in that month before the Nazi Blitz how French officers would explain the magic workings of the Maginot Line. It was a huge underground labyrinth of defence stretching along the frontier, bristling with the latest automatic weapons sunk in impenetrable concrete. Behind this line the French nation lived for years in a dream of invulnerability. And that dream was their undoing when Hitler gave the signal for attack. The fear that built the line was justified, but *l'esprit Maginot* — the myth of invulnerability — made it ultimately useless.

The French are not the only nation to indulge in *the myth of invulnerability*. The sea-ramparts of Britain, the ocean-wide isolation of America have in their turn provoked the sense of utter security. And in more recent years haven't we seen the entire West comfortably covered by the magic cloak of a nuclear supremacy fondly imagined to be permanent ? Now that the world lies open, with every corner vulnerable as never before, now that the nations will soon be peering at one another from some platform in space, now at last we can fold away the magic cloak and stand up like men to make our decisions and set our course in a world that is, and always has been, perilous and insecure.

This is not to say that either nations or individuals must abandon all precautions and expose themselves heedlessly to danger. In a world of bombs and germs and lethal traffic on the roads we have a duty of defence. But we must be rid of the myth of invulner-ability, of faith in some infallible outer protection. Ours is an age of prophylactic obsession—the nuclear shield, the wonder drug, the filter through which no tars can come. Are we seeking the Kingdom of God and His righteousness or some antiseptic paradise where nobody gets hurt ? There is no Garden of Eden to which we can scramble back, for, you remember

" he drove out the man ; and he placed . . . a flaming sword which turned every way." We are out ; and we have a way to go through a world in which there is no infallible shield against its dangers and its risks. It is a world in which the Son of Man " set his face to go to Jerusalem," where no legion of angels came to rescue Him, and where there fell across His shoulders not a magic cloak, but a Cross.

If we are serious about our faith, we are bound to think of the cost of Christian living, the command to take up our own cross and follow Him. This means going out with Him to meet what life may bring, exposed like Him to its pain or danger. But this is not the whole story of the Christian life. We are not simply tossed into a turbulent sea and left to sink or swim. As Christ's followers we are equipped ; we are protected ; we are empowered. He never calls a man or woman to follow Him without bestowing His promise. He does not talk to His followers like a sad and weary martyr, beckoning the way to suffering and despair. Nor does He speak like a noble Stoic, saying : You must grit your teeth and go through with it even if the end be total loss. He speaks as a victorious commander who knows that the enemy's power is broken and can promise an invincible armour for the struggle and the final triumph. " I beheld Satan as lightning fall from heaven. Behold, I give unto you power to tread on serpents and scorpions, and over all the power of the enemy : and *nothing shall by any means hurt you.*"

" Nothing shall by any means hurt you." Did Peter remember this when years later he was writing to some Christians who were in mortal danger ? Spread across what we now call Syria and Turkey at the end of the first century were little colonies of Christians, struggling to hold the faith in a very hostile environment. Like many in our generation they never knew when a knock at the door in the night would be the prelude to arrest, imprisonment, torture or death. And when Peter writes to give advice it is what even a neutral observer would call a very sensible letter. It talks of Christian behaviour in very practical terms. There is nothing fanatical in its tone. He warns these young Christians against getting into unnecessary trouble with their employers or with the State authorities. But he is adamant about the call to unswerving loyalty to Christ, no matter what the cost. And he knows what that may mean. Yet what does he write ? " Who is he that will harm you, if ye be followers of that which is good ? " Here it is— the promise of the living Christ —" Who is he that will harm you ? " There is then for the Christian *a point of invulnerability*.

At the first sight the claim seems quite absurd. " Who can harm me ? " asks the Christian who receives this letter. " I'll tell you, Peter. The guard who marches me off. He can harm me. The judge who sentences me. He can harm me. And the axe that falls, yes, the axe that falls, Peter, that can harm me, don't you think ? "

Peter knows this very well, just as Christ knows the things that can hurt you and me to-day. Yet here are their words : " Who is he that will harm you ? " says Peter. " Nothing shall by any means hurt you," says the Lord. What do they mean ?

We can only understand when we free ourselves from our obsession with the material world and see ourselves as we really are. We are not animated carcasses that are entirely at the mercy of outside events, the helpless victims of storms and germs and bombs. The real " you," the real " me," lies within —responsive, terribly sensitive to all that happens without, but ultimately beyond its reach. And it is within that the real battle takes place—the battle between good and evil. This is the battle of our chief concern. What is wrong with our modern obsession for prophylactic measures is not the desire to seek protection and security from outward peril, but the priority we give to it. There is a Lenten collect in which we pray : " Keep us both outwardly in our bodies, and inwardly in our souls ; that we may be defended from all adversities which may happen to the body, and from all evil thoughts which may assault and hurt the soul." Are we really as desperately concerned about these evil thoughts as we are about a toothache or the Asian flu ? It's here—in the centre —that we really live ; and what happens here is our ultimate concern.

And it is here—within, at the living centre where we know ourselves—that we can know the only invulnerability. There is no magic cloak to be flung over our bodies, but there is a direction of the soul, a road for you and me to travel, that is beyond all hurt and harm. It is the road that Jesus went in union with His Father. When we read of His last days in Jerusalem do we think of Him as a helpless victim of events ? When He is exposed to insult is it He that is harmed ? Do we imagine that the jeers of the crowd have crushed that soul, or that the nails have pierced and broken that trusting spirit ? In the whole sordid scene, He is the Master, not Pilate, or Herod, or the Council of the Sanhedrin. The Resurrection light is already visible even in Gethsemane, in the Roman court, and on the hill of Calvary. Evil, the evil that we so much fear, is abroad in strength and its most murderous weapons are directed at the Son of Man. " But who is he that will harm you, if ye be followers of that which is good ? " They did their worst—the good was crucified —and to-day the whole Church knows that Jesus Christ emerged invulnerable.

Here is the promise, if this is the direction of our souls. If at the inner centre you seek that which is good, if you follow the incarnate goodness that is Christ, if that is the true direction of your soul— —then *you*, the real you, are invulnerable. Nothing from without can touch you. The real battle is within and when that is won, nothing else can ulti- mately threaten us. How vividly Jesus made this point when speaking of outward ceremonies. " Not that which goeth into the mouth defileth a man, but that which cometh out of the mouth, this defileth a man." The outside things pass through, but " out of the heart proceed evil thoughts, murders, adulteries, fornications, thefts, false witness, blasphemies. These are the things which defile a man." To be cleansed within, to be followers of that which is good, is the top priority. When that is our direction then " who is he that will harm you ? "

The best men and women of all ages have known this to be true—inside and outside the Christian tradition. " No harm can befall a good man," said Socrates, " either in life or after death." And

Shakespeare's Brutus, in the best Stoic tradition, says :

> " There is no terror, Cassius, in your threats ;
> For I am arm'd so strong in honesty
> That they pass by me as the idle wind,
> Which I respect not."

But for us there is a real problem here. How can I be sure of " following that which is good ? " And isn't there something smug and self-satisfied in being so sure that I am " armed in honesty ? " The Christian position is not that we can win for ourselves an invulnerable position. It is conferred on us by God. We follow that which is good, not because we are good, but because Christ is—and He has called us to follow just as we are.

There is therefore no aristocracy of the soul which reaches this invulnerability, leaving the rest of us floundering in doubt and despair. Christ's promise is absolute, and it is for all. To yield to Him, to follow Him, is to be directed to that which is good —and while we follow in that direction, " who is he that will harm you ? "

There is ultimately only one who can harm us— and that is the traitor within. Peter was not talking in the air. He remembered what it was to stand up before a hostile council entirely unafraid. When he and the other disciples were commanded not to speak or teach in the name of Jesus, he simply answered, " Whether it be right in the sight of God to hearken unto you more than unto God, judge ye. For we cannot but speak the things which we have seen and heard." They could rage and threaten, but nothing from outside could really harm him as he followed

Christ. But he remembered also a day when he had tried to save his skin, when he had been afraid, when he had cursed and denied his Lord. And he never would forget the eyes of the Master as He came from the Judgment Hall and looked at him—looked right into the depth where he had hurt himself.

"And who is he that will harm you, if ye be followers of that which is good ? "—" If ye be followers." This is the only condition. Alone, we are exposed to every blast and naked to every danger. In Christ we are invulnerable—even in the lions' den.

Do you remember the story ? "And the king spake and said to Daniel, O Daniel, servant of the living God, is thy God, whom thou servest continually, able to deliver thee from the lions ? " " My God hath sent his angel, and hath shut the lions' mouths, that they have not hurt me." No one supposes that the believer is literally rescued from every danger to the body : there were Christians enough who felt the lions' claws in Peter's day. But the truth remains that nothing in life or in death, in earth or in hell, in the depth of the atom or the height of outer space can harm *you*—the you that is resting on the love and grace of God. It is not long since I looked at the face of a sufferer going through the last throes of a disease that had pounced from the unknown and apparently wrecked a life still young and promising. It might seem that there was nothing here but tragedy and loss. And yet as I looked at that Christian friend I knew that it was true : " Who is he that will harm you ? " This is the invulnerability that breaks the edge of tragedy and that in the end casts out all fear.

This is the way forward for each of us. Once we recognize that there is no magic cloak to hide us from all possible danger from without we can be set free from interminable worry as to hypothetical disaster. And deep within we can stabilize our souls on the invulnerable Christ.

" Who is he that will harm you, if ye be followers of that which is good ?   But and if ye suffer for righteousness' sake, happy are ye : and be not afraid of their terror, neither be troubled ; But sanctify the Lord God in your hearts."

XVII

THE HIDDEN VICTORY

An Easter Address

" But thanks be to God, which giveth us the victory through our
Lord Jesus Christ."—I COR. XV. 57.

I HEARD not long ago about a young writer who
composed a short story which he believed to be the
best he had ever done. The plot was not exactly
original, but he felt he had created a masterpiece of
realism in what you might call the modern school
of gloom-and-guts. One day he was introduced by a
friend to a very old and wise author and to his delight
was invited to come to his study and read the manu-
script to him. So he found himself seated in a chair
opposite the old man and began to read.

The story was about the only son of a poor widow
who lived in a little country cottage nestling in a
Pennsylvanian valley. One day the boy set out for
New York to seek his fortune, and as he left his mother
said : " Now remember, son, if you ever get into
trouble, no matter how bad it is, you set off home and
as you come over the hill you'll always find a light
burning in this window—and I'll be waiting to welcome
you." The young author then went on to describe
what happened in the big city—and, as you have
guessed, drew a lurid picture of the decline and fall

of his hero, sparing no detail of the debauchery and crime into which he sank. Finally he served a term in prison and, when he came out, decided to make for home and his mother. He hitch-hiked most of the way in the best tradition of the beat-generation, and then finally walked over the hill towards home. As he came over the crest and looked down, there was the outline of the old cottage in the evening gloom, and—there was no light burning. At this point the old author who had listened to the tale leaped to his feet and cried : " You young devil, *put that light back* ! "

Do you ever feel like that when looking at ~~some canvases of contemporary~~ *modern* art, those pictures that often so ~~brilliantly~~ convey the confusion, ~~the~~ brutality, *and* ~~the~~ distortion of the human spirit ? Put that light back ! Or when *you* watching ~~one of these~~ *a* plays where not a single decent motive seems to operate, the characters are uniformly as squalid as the set ? Or when *you* reading a novel whose author seems to agree with the opinion expressed to Gulliver in Brobdingnag : " I cannot but conclude the bulk of you natives to be the most pernicious race of little odious vermin that nature ever suffered to crawl upon the surface of the earth " ? Or perhaps ~~also~~ when *by* listening to sermons that spell out the corruption of mankind with ~~such theological~~ gusto and detailed illustration *so* ~~that you are~~ left wondering why the New Testament message is called Good News ? Artists, writers, philosophers, preachers—we are the experts on sin to-day. Is there no such thing as the grace of God ? Put that light back !

The trouble is that there is a very easy way to put *the* ~~that~~ light back. It's so easy, so appealing, and so

popular, ~~that~~ I'm (not) surprised that serious men and
women will have nothing to do with it.   It's the
Pollyanna philosophy of the Happy Ending.   With
a stroke of the pen our young writer could put the
light back.   It's as easy as that—in fiction.   And it is
entirely possible to create a fictional Happy Ending
for all our troubles.   Look at the theology of Hollywood at work among the masterpieces of tragic art.
No story must end like *Hamlet* with the hero's death
and " the rest is silence."   The script-writer waves his
wand, the hero revives, and the rest is stereophonic
marriage bells.   The ~~American~~ public, ~~in defiance
of the eggheads~~, demands a Happy Ending.   So—
hey-presto !—the Happy Ending is provided.   The
Hollywood theology invades our thinking from every
direction.   Eliminate death and disaster from your
vocabulary.   Pretend they don't exist.   Everything
will turn out for the best.   This is the neon-light that
comes on at a flick of the switch.

To-day, we celebrate the Christian answer to the
merchants of squalor and misery.   Even the most
gloomy and sin-ridden preacher can hardly help putting
the light back on Easter Day.   The rising sun is followed on his course around the world by the jubilation
of a thousand languages with one unanimous refrain :
" Christ is risen ! "   The anxious, listening world hears
again the Christian conviction that the crucified Lord
was not held in the grave, that Christ has conquered
sin and death and is alive for evermore.   " But thanks
be to God, which giveth us the victory through our
Lord Jesus Christ."

You come to worship either because you know that
this is true, or because you wish it were.   And since
all of us are living through days when such a belief

is not just marginal but central, we cannot be content to leave these questions unanswered : Is this Christian faith just another Pollyanna philosophy, the switching on of a fictional light ?   Is the Resurrection story just another version of the Happy Ending ?   Is this victory Paul speaks of a real event or a pious hope ? Let me tell you why I believe that this is the true light, " ~~the master-light of all our seeing,~~ " and that this is a real victory in which we all can share.

1. The narratives of the Resurrection are not tacked on to the New Testament as if some editor could not bear to leave the story at the Cross.   They are an integral part of the story in each Gospel, and each is different in detail.   (An editor would have made his Happy Ending identical in form.)   As we read each Gospel and let the figure of Jesus Christ emerge in His full stature as Lord and Saviour of mankind we discover the seeds of resurrection embedded in the narrative from the beginning.   This is no sob-story of a good man hounded to His death that needs to be given the Hollywood treatment to appease our injured conscience.   Here is One who is perfectly at home in both worlds, and speaks as naturally of heaven as of earth.   Here is One whose every word and action proclaims His mastery over sin and death. Even in His Via Dolorosa, broken, bruised, deserted, He has the victory touch : " Daughters of Jerusalem, weep not for me."   And with His dying breath to the thief on the other cross, speaks a word of resurrection-power : " Verily I say unto thee, To-day shalt thou be with me in paradise."

Easter does not just mean that once upon a time there was a man who rose from the dead.   It means that *this* Man—this Jesus Christ, the Son of God— could not be held within the grave. To such a life the Resurrection comes, not as a fantastic miracle to be invented by His friends, but as the natural climax of a life that is the miracle of miracles—God manifest on earth.

This victory over the grave is not only of one piece with the whole Gospel story : it is the foundation of the entire New Testament. Open any of the letters of Paul, or Peter, or James, or John, and you will find that the infant Church was founded on the fact that Christ is risen, really risen from the dead, and a living power in the world. Men do not stake their lives on a fiction, or go to the arena for a fabricated happy ending. For them Christ rose : the victory was real. And as others listened they too believed.

2. " But thanks be to God, which giveth us the victory through our Lord Jesus Christ." This victory is the outcome of a real struggle with the forces of evil, sin, suffering and death. The Christian Gospel does not pretend that these things do not exist. If I had just Resurrection and no Cross to preach, I might feel that I was offering questionable comfort for the real needs of men. But this Easter message comes to us from the heart of our human agony. It speaks of a victory won—not in some happy-land, far, far away—but here on this blood-stained earth, where we wrestle with our sins, know the fact of evil, endure suffering, and die. *There* is where the Light shines—not from an ivory-tower, but from a Cross.

" But thanks be to God, which giveth us the victory through our Lord Jesus Christ." To understand these words we need to have listened to Paul as he

I.A.P.—11

struggles with the two major problems we have to face : how to achieve the good we really want, and to avoid the evil that we do ; and how to meet the final enemy called death. Will anyone tell me these are not real questions ? And to each he finds a real answer—Jesus Christ, who died for our sins and rose to deliver us. He died our death and poured out His goodness for the healing of the world. And He rose to lift us up to His life eternal. This victory was won on our battlefield. Here, on our earth, in the middle of our human story, came the supreme clash between good and evil, between hatred and love. And when a group of frightened men saw a Risen Lord that Easter morning they knew the strife was over and the victory won.

One of the reasons why the Easter season may not always bring us the solid conviction we long for, why beneath the outward celebration there lurks a serpent doubt, is that we have not taken time to know this Christ who " was born of the Virgin Mary, suffered under Pontius Pilate, was crucified, dead and buried." We have not really watched with Him in the Garden, or stood by Him at the Cross. A religion that leaps from Christmas to Easter is a mere skeleton of faith, a shadowy ghost that cannot bring conviction to our souls. Only when we know the Christ of flesh and blood, the Christ who was tempted, the Christ who fought with sin till His flesh was broken and His blood poured out ; only when we have been touched somewhere in the depths by those solid nails, smelted from the ore of our native earth, by that hard cross shaped from the wood of our own forests ; only then can we know how true it is that Christ is risen from the dead. Only if somehow, somewhere, we have been with Him in the prison-house of pain and sin, can we share the victory that liberates our souls.

3. Where is the victory? That is what men ask. Show me the victory, show me the evidence that the power of sin is broken, and the menace of death removed. If the Easter message brings us the true Light, and not a will-o'-the-wisp of man's devising, why is evil still rampant and why does death still prowl and pounce?

Let me remind you of that Easter morning. The world was waking to a normal day. The housewives were preparing the usual meal, the children waking and getting dressed. In the Governor's Palace Pilate might be signing his reports, in any one of which the name of Jesus would occur. Herod would probably be still sleeping off a night's carousal. Armies would be on the move in Italy and Gaul. Indians would be hunting through the forests of Manhattan. The world was in its usual groove. Millions woke and slept, and ate and drank, and loved and hated, as before. And not more than a few women and two men knew that Christ had risen.

This was a hidden victory. It was made known in the quietest possible way to a group of very ordinary people. We forget that if it had been otherwise God would have destroyed mankind. For a tremendous demonstration of heavenly power, so universal and compelling that all must believe, would have shattered human nature, and we should have ceased to be real, responsive, responsible men and women. But look what happened to those who heard the news! If it had been illusion, make-believe, their witness would have been snuffed out in forty days. Instead it so

gripped men's hearts and passed with secret power
from life to life that soon the victory-news was racing
over the ancient world like a prairie fire. And to this
day the evidence is found, not in the headlines of
the daily press nor in the invincible prestige of a
powerful Church, but in lives where Christ is King,
lives that know the inner working of His Spirit, men
and women who know what it is to say : " O death,
where is thy sting ? O grave, where is thy victory ?
The sting of death is sin ; and the strength of sin is
the law. But thanks be to God, which giveth us the
victory through our Lord Jesus Christ."

John Masefield's poem *The Everlasting Mercy* tells
the story of a drunken poacher—Saul Kane—who
meets with a Quaker girl in a pub, and through her
witness suddenly finds this hidden victory of Christ.
He goes out, as we do, into a world that is identical
with what he knew before. Everything is there in
place as always : there has been no earthquake, no
transforming cataclysm. But to one who has seized
in his heart the secret of the Risen Christ, the world
is truly new. For it is within that the victory has
dawned.

" O glory of the lighted mind.
How dead I'd been, how dumb, how blind.
The station brook, to my new eyes,
Was babbling out of paradise ;
The waters rushing from the rain
Were singing Christ is risen again.
I thought all earthly creatures knelt
From rapture of the joy I felt."

This is the victory offered to you this morning by
the Christian Church : the knowledge that Christ

is the conqueror of sin and death, and the promise of His transforming power. In the middle of our ordinary tasks, right here where we have each our problems and our cares, and our anxious world crowds in on us from day to day, we hear with the inward ear the trumpets of His victory. Let them sound again ! Put that light back ! For there at Calvary and in the Easter Garden the victory was won. And here in the sanctuary it is *given* to you. " In the world ye shall have tribulation," said Jesus, " but be of good cheer ; I have overcome the world." We have troubles enough to contend with and are often threatened with defeat in our souls. " But thanks be to God, which giveth us the victory through our Lord Jesus Christ."

XVIII

INNOCENCE BY ASSOCIATION

" Yet thou sayest, Because I am innocent, surely his anger shall turn from me. Behold, I will plead with thee, because thou sayest, I have not sinned."—JER. II. 35.

"I AM innocent. . . . I have not sinned."
This is a nation speaking. They had had enough of Jeremiah with his continual denunciation of their ingratitude, idolatry and apostasy. He was everywhere—at street-corners, on the city walls, in the council-chambers with his insistent : Thus saith the Lord. Why couldn't he be content, like the priests in the Temple, with keeping the religious machinery going, providing decent services for those who wanted to worship God ? Why had he to drag religion into the everyday life of the nation, its business, its amusements, even its foreign policy ? And so Jeremiah found himself preaching to a brick-wall and his sermons bounced off an impenetrable surface of complacency : " I am innocent. . . . I have not sinned."

This is a nation speaking, and right to this day, this is how a nation always speaks. Everybody knows that there is trouble in the world, violence, bloodshed, persecution, tensions, fears. Yet if you listen to the speeches in the United Nations and believe all that is said, you must find it a complete mystery how such things could be. For every nation in the end makes

158

this same speech—Israel, Egypt, Britain, France, Russia, India, America—" I am innocent. . . . I have not sinned." Yes; somebody is lying—but it is always the other fellow.

In our sober moments we must know perfectly well that there is no such thing as an innocent nation. There are, of course, degrees of guilt, and we have no right to paralyse judgment on an international crime simply because no one is entirely innocent. But the illusion of innocence is a powerful one. We like to feel that our country is the immaculate one pursuing a virtuous and altruistic course in a world of cunning and rapacious foreigners.

The same thing happens in any smaller community —in a home, an office, a society. Trouble breaks out around some principle or personality. And immediately everyone involved becomes a model of innocence. " A has the wrong attitude ; B is an impossible person ; C began it all . . ." " *I* am innocent . . . *I* have not sinned." How easily we convince ourselves of our complete integrity and lay the entire blame elsewhere. I once saw a play in Edinburgh, based on an actual incident. It concerned two sisters who shared a large room in a tenement. At the time of the Disruption in the Church they found themselves on opposite sides. The argument broke out ; words flew ; and eventually they drew a chalk line down the middle of the room. From then on each lived on her own side of the line—and cooked, washed, dressed and received visitors as if the other didn't exist. Each felt certain " I am innocent. . . . I have not sinned." So long as that conviction lasted the dividing-line was a reality for them both.

And that dividing-line will continue to run through

families and societies and nations so long as the claim
of innocence dominates the soul of man. For our claim
to be innocent always means passing the blame to
someone else. And when blame is passed human relations are poisoned, for blame is a virus that circulates.
From the vicious circle of blame there seems to be no
escape. To-day we have become more sophisticated
and don't always automatically pass on the blame to
certain people. We have found other ways of proving
our innocence. If I have a desire to kick my neighbour's dog, or swindle the Income Tax authorities, I
can lay the blame on the urge of my ancestors, or the
secretions of my glands. " I am innocent. . . . I have
not sinned." We call science to the rescue—psychology, sociology, biology—all the perfumes of our modern
Arabia to sweeten this little hand. But, in effect, we
are shifting the blame. " I am innocent. . . . I have
not sinned."

What a strange and dynamic drive this is to establish
innocence ! Wouldn't you think that a generation
that has to a great extent thrown off the obligations
of religion ought to be free of this compulsion ? A
student will tell you that he is persuaded that there is
no God to hold us to account, no standards of right
and wrong that have any validity beyond social use-
fulness—and then you will find him plunged into some
frantic activity to alleviate the guilt he feels about
something that happened in China, in Hungary, or
in Hiroshima. And nations—even nations that are
avowedly atheistic—will commit no crime without
a simultaneous effort to establish innocence in the
eyes of the world. Hypocrisy has been called " the
tribute paid by vice to virtue " : it is also a tribute to
the urge to innocence.

What light does the Bible throw on this problem ? Have we in the Church any resources for understanding this compulsion that we feel, this desire to be cleared, to be clean, to be blameless ?

There are two kinds of innocence of which the Bible speaks.

1. The first is *the innocence of Adam.* This is set in the beginning of our Bibles, not as a piece of history to tell us about the origins of the human race, but as a prologue about Man—a story to tell us about ourselves. Adam is the Hebrew word for " man." This is about you and me. The curtain goes up on man and woman in a garden. Everything is new and pure and happy. In one corner stands the Tree of Knowledge, of Good and Evil—untouched. For Adam and Eve are innocent, and theirs is the innocence of ignorance. This Eden—this Garden of innocence—is planted deep in the human heart, an image of a state to which we long to return. It is, if you like, the innocence and ignorance of the womb—or as the poet sees it, a heaven that is our origin.

" Not in entire forgetfulness,
　And not in utter nakedness,
　But trailing clouds of glory do we come
　From God, who is our home."

The innocence of Adam—isn't that what we try to establish—the childlike innocence—the innocence that did not know ? But what happens to Adam ; what happened to us ? Our eyes were opened. We knew. And with knowledge came choice. And with choice also choice of evil. The gates of Eden closed. That is the story. With a clang of utter finality the gates closed on the Garden of innocence, and there was no way back. " And he placed at the east of the garden of Eden Cherubims, and a flaming sword which turned every way, to keep the way of the tree of life."

This is what we find it hard to accept—that we have passed the point of no return, that we are adult human beings already committed, already knowing good and evil, and already with the record of sin behind us. Look at Adam and Eve in their attempt to scramble back. " And he said . . . Hast thou eaten ? " " And the man said, The woman . . . she gave me of the tree." " And the woman said, The serpent beguiled me, and I did eat." It has begun. Pass the blame. " *I* am innocent. . . . *I* have not sinned."

There is no way back to the innocence of Adam. The flaming sword is still there, barring the way. The old game of passing the blame only leads us farther and farther into the toils of the vicious circle. We stand responsible. We cannot isolate ourselves from the cry of distress that reaches us from any distant corner of the human family. We are like the courtiers who brought about the downfall of Richard II, and his voice is the voice that speaks to our conscience whenever we feel like claiming " It is not my fault : "

" Though some of you with Pilate wash your hands,
   Showing an outward pity ; yet you Pilates
   Have here deliver'd me to my sour cross,
   And water cannot wash away your sin."

2. These words bring us straight to that other innocence of which the Bible speaks : *the innocence of Christ*.

If the Bible opens with the legend of Eden, it centres

on the historic fact of Christ. Who is this that appears in the middle of our human story and what can He do to help us in our plight ? He doesn't come to any Eden of our dreams, but to this solid world we know —a world where men lived, and loved and hated, and laughed and cried ; a world where nations jostled for power, and men for gold ; a world where people like you and me were trying to make sense out of a scrambling and confusing struggle for existence. And this Jesus moved out into this world with the innocence of God upon His brow. His first public action was to go to the place where men and women whose conscience was awake were acknowledging their sins and seeking to be cleansed in the waters of baptism. And when John, who at first had wanted to stop Him, saw this innocent Christ in the waters with sinners, he suddenly sensed that a new power, a new contagious innocence was abroad in the world. " Behold the Lamb of God —the innocent one—which taketh away the sin of the world."

That first scene was a symbol of what followed. From the Jordan to Nazareth, from Nazareth to Galilee, from Galilee to Jerusalem, this Man passed through our world of light and shade, hope and despair —and was everywhere uncontaminated by sin. This was not the innocence of Adam, the innocence of ignorance. He, too, was tempted in all points as we are, yet without sinning. The people said : " He hath done all things well." He said : " Which of you convinceth me of sin ? " Pilate said : " I can find in him no fault at all," and the soldier who watched Him die said : " Certainly this was a righteous man." Jesus Christ was innocent—in the full knowledge of an adult man, He was innocent, in the midst of sin,

He was innocent, dying the death of a common criminal, He was innocent.

And what does that mean for us? Nothing at all, if this was just a demonstration—God sending His Son to show how we should live. But it was not just a demonstration. It was a deliverance. The Son of God was not sent as an example but as a Rescuer. He came to the rescue of people like you and me with our involvement in evil, and the fears that rise from the conscience that accuses. For this innocence of Christ is a contagious, infectious innocence. It was a new and realistic innocence that met man at the very point where he cried to be delivered. It was an amazing, vicarious innocence of love, absorbing the sins of mankind. For in a world where evil was rampant; and where the people blamed the Pharisees, and the Pharisees blamed the Sadducees, and the Sadducees blamed Herod, and all blamed the Romans; where parents blamed children and children blamed parents, the innocent Christ went calmly to the Cross saying: " *I'll* take the blame." And in the darkness on that innocent head fell the great weight of human shame and sin. " All we like sheep have gone astray; we have turned everyone to his own way; and the Lord hath laid on him the iniquity of us all."

How can this innocence of Christ become effective for us? Only as we cease to claim the innocence of Adam, cease struggling to maintain our status before God, cease beating our heads against these gates that are closed. We have the choice—to stand with Pilate washing our hands and saying: " I am innocent of the blood of this just person," or with the thief on the other cross to say, " Lord, remember me." For such a word is enough. This is the only innocence we can have, the innocence that God is willing to bestow upon us for the sake of His Christ. It comes by our association with Him. This innocence is not a return to Eden ; it is an innocence that comes to cleanse us where we are and to clothe us for the fight we have still to wage.

" Behold," says God, " I will plead with thee, because thou sayest, I am innocent." Yes, He has come to plead with us, to show us the only innocence we can attain, to bring to us an absolute assurance of forgiveness for all our sins and acceptance as sons and daughters of His love. This is the power that cuts the vicious circle. For as we are associated with Christ, sharing His innocence, we are enabled to forgive as we have been forgiven. And this is the way of hope, the way of life, for a tormented world.

XIX

CHRISTIAN MAINTENANCE

" Let us not allow slackness to spoil our work and let us keep the fires of the spirit burning as we do our work for God."—ROM. XII. 11 (Phillips).

" There once was a man with a very fine car,
Which no one had ever seen go very far.
When asked to explain he would sadly reply :
' You can't understand it, and neither can I ;
For ten years ago she was tuned, and they greased her,
And I fill her with gas every Christmas and Easter ' ! "

MAINTENANCE : that was his trouble. We have learned that nothing—from ~~automobiles~~ *no on car* to washing-machines, ~~to golf-handicaps~~—can be kept in condition without maintenance. We know that a talent for playing the piano, or singing, or ~~figure~~ *ice*-skating, can be preserved only by constant practice. Yet somehow we allow ourselves to imagine that our most precious possession, our greatest talent, the most difficult art of all—Christian faith and life—can be kept up without any ~~particular trouble.~~ *real effort*

" Is your Daddy a Christian ? " asked the little boy. " Yes," said his friend, " but he's not been doing much about it ~~recently.~~" *later That kid hit a nail on the head*

~~That's just it.~~ We don't often think of our Christianity as a matter we should be " doing something

166

about." We've ~~made our basic decisions~~ been baptized, confirmed, and have assumed certain Church responsibilities—and then we are inclined to sit back. We rather expect to be carried along somehow on a tide that will see us through any passing *storms* ~~squalls~~, and deposit us eventually on some eternal shore.

~~I say " we " not as an oblique way of getting at any special group of people. When I say " we " I mean " we " for I know as well as anybody how easy it is~~ *We* ~~to~~ take our Christian life for granted and to rely on being carried by our past experience or the continuing life of the Church.~~ We do not like to face the ~~sober~~ truth that as Christians we are swimming against the tide, and, if we stop, nothing on earth can prevent us *from* drifting *in* the wrong way. You and I are either better Christians than we were a year ago—or worse. The Bible tells us, and our own experience *confirms it* ~~tells us, that~~ we cannot drift towards the Kingdom of God. The world-the-flesh-and-the-devil may be an out-of-date expression but they are terribly up-to-date realities for those who care about their religion. Our Christian faith is confronted by the forces of unbelief, not usually in flaming headlines but in a thousand subtle pressures on our mind. Our Christian life is threatened by pagan ~~and sub-Christian~~ standards that we sometimes hardly notice while they nibble at the edges of our convictions. When we realize that there is no Christian cushion to fall back on in this world ~~we live in~~, and that we have to be alert and mobile if our faith is to be alive, then we begin to understand why the Bible and the hymn-books are so fond of the metaphors of war. The fight is on. We must look to our spiritual *weapons* ~~armament~~, the maintenance of our Christian

faith. In other words we have to " do something
about it." ⟶ *Physio*

Now   It would be so simple if someone would prescribe
for us a set of spiritual exercises by which our religious vitality could be guaranteed. If " doing something about it " could be defined as performing X
number of devotional acts per week, with results
guaranteed, most of us could probably be bullied into
line. But we have only to open the New Testament to
discover that our salvation cannot be earned by something that we do, and that the Christian life is too
dynamic and pervasive to be achieved by religious
rule. ~~As Protestants we stand by the Word which~~
~~says : " By *grace* are ye saved through faith "~~ and
~~the Easter message of a victory that is *given* and not~~
~~won by us.~~ How then do we meet the challenge of
Christian maintenance, and do battle with the forces
that would drag us down ?

We have misunderstood this message of God's
grace if we imagine that it absolves us from all effort
and responsibility for the maintenance of faith.
Dietrich Bonhoeffer, the young German theologian
who defied the world-the-flesh-and-the-devil when they
wore the uniform of the Gestapo, and faced a firing
squad in utter confidence in the grace of God, ~~has~~ left
some timely words ~~for us~~ about what he calls " cheap
grace." The grace of God, offered freely to us all in
the death and resurrection of Jesus Christ, can indeed
deliver us from sin, and liberate us from the yoke of
religious bondage—but woe unto us if we take it for
granted. " Cheap grace " is our assumption that,
no matter what we do, or don't do, all will be well
with our souls. " Cheap grace " is the commodity
we traffic in when we settle for that modicum of

faith and love we have already known. " Cheap grace " is that imaginary cushion where we try to rest our souls while we get on with other things.

Our text is taken from the Phillips' translation of the twelfth chapter of Romans, not because I think that anything can yet replace the majesty and power of the King James version in our public worship, but because this passage should be heard afresh with the kind of impact that it must have had on those Christian ancestors of ours in first-century Rome. It's a piece of straight exhortation to the Christian life, clear and crisp as battle-orders. And, remember, it comes at the end of the most massive exposition of God's free grace in Christ the world has ever heard. Paul has spoken of the death and resurrection of Jesus Christ as the mighty acts of God on which our salvation rests, in words that have leaped to life again whenever the Gospel has been smothered by the routines of the Church. Augustine, Luther, Wesley, Karl Barth in our own day—all these and many others were roused to rouse the Church by this letter to the Romans. Yet it is just here, not in spite of, but because of, his passionate conviction that God has given us the victory, that Paul reminds us that there is something for us to do.

" Let us not allow slackness to spoil our work and let us keep the fires of the spirit burning as we do our work for God." Here is a warning and an incentive. After the great affirmations of the Gospel come the sharp imperatives to the Christian flock. There is no contradiction here. A human family, such as we all have known, is, after all, founded on the great affirmation of parental love, and held together by a grace that is bestowed upon us, but that does not rule out the occasional and timely imperative. Our parents' commands were not the basis of our family life—but we know how often we needed them ! So it is in God's family. He brings us into it by His act of love, He holds us in it by His grace, but from time to time He has to speak to us the sharp reminders that we need if we are to maintain the faith and have our vision sharpened for the way ahead.

" Let us not allow slackness to spoil our work." *That is the warning.* The King James version translates these words : " not slothful in business "—a rhythmic phrase that has often been used as a kind of Christian incentive in the world of commerce. However apt this may be it is not what the apostle had in mind. He wasn't giving a pep-talk to tired businessmen. The " business " he means is " the Lord's business "—our total Christian witness and behaviour, wherever we are, whatever our work.

" Let us not allow slackness to spoil our work." Slackness. Somehow we don't associate slackness with those early Christians in Rome. We think of them meeting for worship in secret places at the risk of their lives, scratching their names and texts on the walls of the catacombs, going singing into the arena to meet the lions. Yet these were the people the apostle is warning about slackness and sloth. I wonder how much more keenly he might feel that we needed such a word !

How well the Bible knows us. Slackness is exactly the temptation to which an evangelical Christian is exposed. Our church is, we believe, solidly founded on the Word of God and the Sacraments of His grace.

We believe in the freedom of the Christian to make his own response, and no one checks whether or not we confess our sins, or say our prayers. Our devotional practices are not prescribed for us, and even the discipline exerted by our forefathers has largely fallen into disuse. The apostle might well say to us : " Yes, you've learned pretty well what I told the Romans about the free grace of God. You know that you can't buy your salvation by pious practices. You're very sure that outward forms are worthless without an inner faith. You've found something of the freedom of the Gospel—don't ever bargain it away. But— have you my other word ? Have you realized that this freedom is not something to be smugly tucked away, but a trumpet-call to action ? that when you allow no man to dictate your devotions there is a stronger obligation laid upon you ? that when there is no rule imposed from without the inner discipline has to be so much the stronger ? Are you really at work as a Christian ? Do you regularly pray ? Do you fulfil the vows you freely took ? Let us not allow slackness to spoil our work."

The Church Fathers were right when they included slackness as one of the Seven Deadly Sins. For many of us it is more deadly than any of the other more exciting and picturesque vices. It quietly undermines all our resolutions, but never seems quite vicious enough to warrant our feeling really penitent. Call it " sloth " and the word suggests an old-fashioned laziness that we may not recognize, but give it its modern name and we know it very well. When I carried out a parish visitation once in Scotland and entered many homes where nominal church members had not been seen around the church for a long time,

I was rather surprised at what I heard. I expected to hear expressions of doubt as to what the Church was teaching, or criticisms of how the Church was acting. Instead, usually without any prompting whatever, I heard something like this : " I'd like to come to church again : I'm afraid I just got a bit slack." If we were to pause now and think, I believe each one of us could think of some area in our Christian life where the whole trouble is that we've just got a bit slack. That's all—and isn't it enough to make us think ?

For here is one sin that we can most certainly do something about. That's why our text speaks so directly about it. We do not require vast supernatural aid to put this right. It isn't as if we had to await a heavenly vision or an upsurge of spiritual power. I once heard Dr. Graham Scroggie, who was a magnificent exponent of the liberating power of Christ and the Gospel promises of victory, tell of how a lady came to see him with a special problem. " Dr. Scroggie," she said, " I want you to tell me how to get victory over my tendency to lie in bed too long in the morning." " Madam," he said, " I advise you to put one leg over the bed and draw the other after it." We sometimes go looking for some so-called " spiritual experience " when God is talking directly to our wills and common sense.

" Let us not allow slackness to spoil our work— and let us keep the fires of the spirit burning as we do our work for God." " The fires of the spirit." *Here is the incentive.* The element of sheer will-power that can overcome our slackness is not the whole story. Our Christian maintenance does not depend solely on our being prodded into action. God *is* at

work within. If we have *he have* in any way, yielded our life
to Christ the fires of His spirit are burning. If we
have truly sought Him, even if we are terribly doubtful
and confused, the fires of His spirit are burning. It
may be a long time since you felt an active glow of
faith, strong enough to impel you into what Paul
calls " our work for God," but the fires are still burning.
When the prophet Isaiah drew his picture of God's
coming King, he had this to say about Him : " A
bruised reed shall he not break, and smoking flax
shall he not quench." Our ancestors knew what
it was to have a hearth with a fire that never went
out. So long as there was smoke there was potential
fire to be kindled to a blaze. There are men and
women to-day, apparently without interest in this
" work for God," who carry within them this smoking flax. A text from the Bible, a hymn that stirs
old memories, an accident or sudden loss, an
unexpected word from a friend—and the fire flickers
into life.

" Let us keep the fires of the spirit burning as we do
our work for God." How? Well, we know very well
what keeps a fire burning and what puts it out. Fuel
and air will keep it going : water and suffocation will
extinguish it. And we know very well what keeps the
fires of the spirit burning, and what is likely to quench
them. There are habits, practices, places, people,
books, music, patterns of our thoughts, which we know
from experience are as fuel and air for the fires of the
spirit within. And we know equally well what tends to
suffocate and quench. Why do you think we pray :
Lead us not into temptation ? Christian maintenance
can sometimes depend quite simply on the atmosphere
we choose to breathe.

There are high seasons in the Christian Year when even the slackest are roused and the strong winds of faith blowing across the world from Bethlehem or Calvary stir the smoking fires to life. But the work for God which clamours to be done in our generation will not be served by a sporadic devotion or a seasonal faith. Christian maintenance is a year-round job, and these coming months are a good test of our will to respond. It was with the future months and years in mind that Jesus said to Peter : " I have prayed for thee, that thy faith fail not." And this same Christ makes that prayer for us to-day. " Let us not allow slackness to spoil our work for the Lord and let us keep the fires of the spirit burning as we do our work for God."

Let me close with John Bunyan's picture of the nourishing of that inner fire :

" Then I saw in my dream that the Interpreter took Christian by the hand and led him into a place where there was a fire burning against a wall, and one standing by it, always casting much water upon it to quench it ; yet did the fire burn higher and hotter.

" Then said Christian, What means this ?

" The Interpreter answered, This fire is the work of grace that is wrought in the heart ; he that casts water upon it to extinguish and put it out, is the devil : but in that thou seest the fire notwithstanding burn higher and hotter, thou shalt also see the reason of that. So he had him about to the backside of the wall, where he saw a man with a vessel of oil in his hand, of the which he did also continually cast (but secretly) into the fire.

" Then said Christian, What means this ?

" The Interpreter answered, This is Christ, who

continually, with the oil of his grace, maintains the work already begun in the heart : by the means of which, notwithstanding what the devil can do, the souls of his people prove gracious still."

" This is Christ," and this is what He is doing for us.

XX

OUR LINK WITH THE ETERNAL

" And this is the record, that God hath given to us eternal life, and this life is in his Son."—I JOHN V. 11.

"I LOVE my life," said a man lying in a hospital bed. " I love all of it—my home, my friends, the countryside, the city, children playing in the street, dogs and kittens, even the noise of new buildings going up. I love it all—and now I'm beginning to say to myself : ' You're not going to have it much longer '." This wasn't a complaint : it was a good, healthy, sensible point of view. We're meant to love life like this, to savour to the full the good things God has given us. I think the best grave-stone inscription I ever saw was in a village in Denmark. It consisted of these words : " Tak for Alt "—" Thanks for everything." Isn't that the right note on which to pass the Great Divide ? We're meant to enjoy this world and be thankful. We're also meant to remember, " I'm not going to have it much longer," and the sooner in life we begin to remember this the better.

How can we bring these two thoughts together—that life is good, and that one day, any day, it's going to end ? Lots of people don't want to bring them together. They concentrate on the enjoyment of what life has to offer, and drive the knowledge of its terminus right down out of sight. This may work all right when we're young, and even fifty is a distant horizon of great age. But we're never quite safe, even when very young, from these sharp reminders of mortality that stab into every home and heart, and when we're past the middle years—then we don't need anyone to tell us, " You're not going to have it much longer." In this matter the irreligious man is often a self-deceiver, and the Christian is the realist. For the Christian message takes full account of the fact of death, and the Christian Year of worship together makes special place for its consideration. And it is in the Christian Gospel that these two facts—life is good ; life comes to an end—are brought together, and held together in one full and satisfying truth.

That truth is expressed in the words " eternal life." Unfortunately this is an expression that for many people has been drained of all meaning. " Eternal life ? You mean the idea that when we die we some-how manage to go on existing somewhere, somehow, for ever and ever ? I haven't the slightest idea if this is true, and if it were I don't know that it would interest me. It's *this* life I like, and I hate leaving it for some hypothetical non-stop existence out there." So, at first sight, the words " eternal life " don't seem much of an answer to the problem. They are like that old bottle of pink medicine we've kept on a back shelf for years in case some day it might be useful, although now we've forgotten what it's meant to do.

Suppose we find some other expression to denote what our Bibles call " eternal life." After all, these books were not written in English and our words often fail to communicate the real meaning. The Greek word translated " eternal " means something different from just going on and on. It describes another *kind* of life, not just a lot more of the same. It's life, as we know it, with something extra to it, with another dimension in it. How can life have something extra ? Well, I think we would all agree that men and women share life with the animals. Like them we eat and sleep and mate. But we have this common life plus something extra. Locate it where you will—in the power of thought, or speech, or conscious creation—there is an extra to human life, unknown to the animals. Then why can there not be a possible extra to ordinary human life, that which is not bound to the limitations of time and space, a dimension which we may know that transcends the normal routine of human existence ? This is the quality we are thinking about. Instead of " eternal life " let's call it " Life-plus."

Where is this Life-plus to be found and how do we get hold of it ?

There is a plain answer in the Bible, and it's backed by the conviction and experience of the entire Christian Church. "And this is the record, that God hath given us ' life-plus,' and this life is in his Son."

This is the record. It's what we need to hear. The apostle is speaking to those who are Christians, and his message is as clear for us to-day as when it first rang out across the shivering paganism of the Graeco-Roman world.

" God has given us Life-plus." Eternal life, to use the familiar expression, is then something that we possess *now* if we are believers, and not what has been called " pie in the sky when we die." Right here and now, in the middle of this world of every-day, this life that, with all its problems, we enjoy so much—right here and now another world is pressing in upon us, the world of God. And to live in that world is to have Life-plus. It means to be awake to the world of God while living in the world of men— more than that, it is to realize that the *true* world of men is the world of God. " This is the record, that God hath given us—here and now—eternal life " this Life-plus, and we can learn to see our daily life, not just in the dull dimensions of time and space, but with the stereoscopic vision of eternity.

If this is to be anything more than a beautiful theory, if we are truly to enter into this Life-plus, we need to realize afresh those links that bind us to the eternal world. Only then can we begin to see why the Christian can truly love and be thankful for the life that now surrounds us, while calmly accepting the brute fact of death. What matters is not so much that we try to convince ourselves that there is a heaven to come, as that we strengthen these ties that bind to the heaven that is here. For the more really and genuinely we know Life-plus as a present experience the more surely do we draw the sting from death.

In the last great act of Shakespeare's *Antony and Cleopatra*, the Queen prepares for the end. Decked in the symbols of her former glory she awaits a world where they have little worth :

" Give me my robe, put on my crown ; I have
  Immortal longings in me."

Deep within each one of us there are these " immortal longings," the knowledge that we were not born for death. In our most solemn moments we have all felt the tug of the eternal, those moments when time stands still and we know that behind this passing scene there *is* a mysterious plus to life. McNeil Dickson in his book *The Human Situation* speaks of these " immortal longings " as being in themselves an indication that they can find fulfilment, and draws a comparison with the life of the womb : " As in the darkness, in the organism not yet born, the eye is formed to correspond to things invisible, and thus with confidence anticipates a world to come, so the soul's faculties, for love, for joy, for admiration, for achievement, correspond to a reality which exists, and is by them foretold. The soul does not provide itself with a passport for an imaginary country, and cannot vibrate to a note unsounded by the universe."

When we are most truly living by the best we know, where, in fact, are our deepest joys in life ? Are they in the passing pleasures of possession, the things we buy, the meals we eat, the clothes we wear ? Or are they not rather located in the love we have known, the beauty we have experienced, the truth we have discovered ? Love and truth and beauty do not share the decay that condemns all earthly things. The truth in a great book is not tied to the perishable paper on which it is written ; the beauty of a symphony does not vanish as the instruments are packed in their cases, the love of another does not die when their mortal remains are laid away. These are links that bind us to the eternal, and when they are strengthened we know that we are in touch with the world everlasting.

Yes ; God has given us eternal life, this Life-plus here and now, and the more fully we receive it, the more steadily we hold out our hands for more, the surer and calmer will be our approach to the moment when we shall not have " all this." For the Christian, then, it is not simply a question of " All this—and heaven too " but " All this—with heaven in it *now*."

Yes ; there are sufficient links, sufficient " intimations of immortality " to throw a transforming light on this daily life of ours, but God's gift to us goes further. If eternal life is life in Him, if Life-plus is really life with God, then we do well to seek the strongest ties with Him. That is why we create a pool of silence in these throbbing lives where we may pray and worship, both alone and together as a family of believers. When we do that we become aware, not only that God is alive and at work in His world, but that He has made this transient physical world the vehicle of His grace. When we truly worship we know that the eternal world is meeting us in the life of everyday. And when we reach the supreme secret of the Christian faith we realize that God Himself, the eternal God, has made the supreme and final link between our life and His. For " this is the record, that God hath given us eternal life, and *this life is in his Son*." The life, the death, the resurrection of Jesus Christ—this is the divine life, the eternal life, the Life-plus, breaking into the world of men. God comes as a man to men, the eternal stoops to the temporal, the holy to the human, the spiritual to the material, and reaches right down to the last degradation and final catastrophe of death, in order that we might be lifted up to Him. The whole power of the eternal, this Life-plus that surges and beats upon the shores of this mortal world, is concentrated in Jesus Christ, who entered our world, died for our sins, and rose again to lift us up to God. This, for the

Christian, is the supreme link here and now with the eternal. In the words of His last great prayer : " This is life eternal, that they might know thee the only true God, and Jesus Christ, whom thou hast sent."

To know Christ now is to have this Life-plus, and so to know Christ now is to know Him then— when this mortal heart has ceased to beat and our eyes open on another and richer world. Of all the links that must now be strengthened this is the most vital. " What if this present were the world's last night ? " cries John Donne,

" Mark in my heart, O Soul, where thou dost dwell,
    The picture of Christ crucified . . ."

There is no other that can so confer upon us the assurance of eternity, a Life-plus that begins right now and passes on beyond into the fullness of that life to come. For in Him is the divine compassion that meets us now and will welcome us then.

THE END